I0221903

Go Be Great!
Overcome and WIN!

Where do I begin to describe to you how Travis has impacted my life? He TRULY helped me discover so many possibilities within myself with just a few moments of his time. I was in a disheartening situation where I had no one else to call. The funny thing about it, too, is that Travis and I barely knew one another. But I felt drawn to reach out to him for help. I told him I was struggling to find myself. He simply told me, no, you aren't struggling to find yourself because yourself doesn't need to be found. He taught me how to define myself. From that moment forward I decided who I wanted to be despite my background or whatever I went through in life. He told me to be who I want to be. I have held onto those few words ever since. Thank you, Travis for your guidance and ability to instill confidence where I saw none.

— *C. Hall, Washington D.C*

From initially meeting Travis, I knew he was an admirable guy. I had no idea at that moment, that he would come to influence many of the decisions that I have made in life, and viewpoints I have grown to know second nature.

I proudly say, I look up to Travis for all that he has and will strive for, and the determination he has to succeed. Travis is dedicated to enriching the lives of those around him, with his electrifying ambition. Travis has managed to balance being a student, a dedicated father, a full-time employee, the founder of a community service-based brotherhood and a mentor for young men. As if that wasn't enough, he goes to work every day to protect his city.

Travis consistently motivates me to strive for my full potential. In witnessing Travis balance the world on his shoulders I too believed, I could ask for the weight of the world and bare it. I became a student leader, a resident assistant, and with a referral from Travis, a full-time employee. Till this day I walk with this ambition, and zeal for purpose. I know that I am a better person for knowing him.

— *C. Jaggon, Brooklyn, NY*

Go Be Great!
Overcome and WIN!

Travis T. Wolfe

WolfeMpowerment^{SM}
PUBLISHING

2016

Copyright © 2017 by Travis T. Wolfe

All rights reserved. This book or any portion thereof may not be reproduced or used in any manner whatsoever without the express written permission of the publisher except for the use of brief quotations in a book review or scholarly journal.

First Printing: 2017

ISBN 978-0-9982752-0-8

Published in Philadelphia by WolfeMpowerment Group

2417 Welsh Rd | Suite 21 | #337

Philadelphia, PA 19114

www.WolfeMpowerment.com

Email: info@WolfeMpowerment.com

Library of Congress Control Number: 2017900930

Dedication

To my wife, Diana, my children Aniya, Travis, Jr., and Ariel. You are my greatest inspiration and support. I love you unconditionally.

And to Police Inspector Steven R. Saymon. In 1992, you showed me the example of a great man. I will ensure your legacy lives on.

Contents

Acknowledgements

I'd be remiss if I did not first acknowledge that I AM grateful to God for allowing me this victory, for affording me the opportunity to do his will, and for blessing me with the courage to do so, unapologetically.

I must acknowledge my beautiful, brilliant, humble, powerful and loving wife, Diana. Thank you for your understanding, tolerance and love throughout this process. This book, my company, my life, our family, my world as I know it would be nothing without you. I love you with every bit of my soul.

To Travis Jr., my son; your abundance of love and your desire to help others are two of my greatest inspirations. Aniya, my princess; your greatness is inspiring to all and your success is one of my greatest motivations. Ariel, my precious little girl, no anger, fear, frustration nor doubt could endure your pure love. You bring everlasting joy to our family and your light is brighter than all the stars of the universe.

To Sarina Wolfe, my baby sister; thank you for inspiring and encouraging me to achieve greatness even when I doubted myself. Thank you for pushing me when I was afraid to jump. Tiona and Ciara, thank you for all your contributions and encouragement, and for fielding all 3,215,619 of my calls that helped confirm my recollection of the occurrences in our lives.

Tracey and Warren, my Mom and Dad—had it not been for you, I would not be the man I am today. Aside from God, I AM grateful for you more than anyone, for, none of this would have been possible without you. I know at times; it may appear that I am painting a terrible picture of you. To be clear, you are indeed, great individuals, today, but my truth is my truth and I must be transparent with the world if I'm going to help to change it. I could never have asked for better parents. Thank you, both for your contributions to the book. I love you.

Dr. Stanley El — You're an angel sent by God to enlighten and guide me through many endeavors in my life. I AM grateful for your mentorship, spiritual guidance, help with the book, the cover, my company, and your unconditional love for me and my family. You have been a great light in my life and in the lives of many others in the world. You are one of the most phenomenal individuals I have ever met.

Olga El — My editor. You took on a great task, indeed. Amid some resistance, somehow you were successful in helping my normally long-winded self to get to the point and ensure this publication was as great as its title. Thank you for your input and suggestions.

Thank you to everyone who's ever believed in me or blessed me with encouraging words.

Foreword

GO BE GREAT! What can be more obvious as a call to put GOD into action? Only GOD is Great and each and every individual is born into that greatness.

Travis Wolfe discovered what it takes to be great. He is compelled to inspire each reader to strive for the impossible, scale the mountain tops, breakdown the barriers and go beyond seeming burdensome limitations.

Meeting and working with Travis, I have been able to reflect on Life, through his mission, as a profound opportunity to prove Life's limitless power. "The clouds have darkened and the thunder and the lightning roared, but the Heavens did not fall."

We all seemed to have come upon dark days in our lives, but somehow we persist. According to Travis, persistence is only the beginning. He says we must think big; acknowledge Victory from the start; and refuse to lose.

The Law of Life is that whatever you hold your attention upon will manifest in your Life experience. We indeed 'reap what we sow.' Know that Life is a power; the greatest power in the Universe and it is in YOU!

Travis demonstrates the Power of Life in this book. He conveys many of the so-called secrets of mastering worldly existence; all for a higher purpose; a reason to be happy, joyous, prosperous and yet still be a good person.

What more can a person ask for? In this book is a story of a hopeless beginning. With the accounts told are keys to giving life fully; with great expectations.

I would never feel at ease if I didn't urge you to delve into this book with a clear set of eyes; with the inner ears listening to the voice of reason. Once you're through reading this book ask yourself, "Am I any different from Travis Wolfe?" The honest answer will most likely be, "No." Then, you can acclaim, "If he can do it, I can."

Yes, all can achieve their dreams. Just be grateful to GOD and the individual He chose to live out their life, regardless of conditions, to become one of the few with the desire to share what it takes to "GO BE GREAT!"

Dr. Stanley El, D.Div.

Introduction

SUCCESS is... *completely* subjective. Before we get started, in the back of this book, answer this: What does success look like to you?

My name is Travis—and I'm a WINNER! I used to be just a poor kid from west Philadelphia. Even though life is great for me now, there was once a time in my life when I was completely downtrodden and destitute. With a gun in my mouth, I found myself praying for mercy. Homelessness, hopelessness, helplessness and hunger endangered my very existence.

In this book, you'll learn of my struggles as a troubled, impoverished youth, raised by a single mother until placed in the foster care system by my own family. You'll learn of my traumatic experiences that include drug addicted parents, child abuse, sexual assault and near-death. You'll learn what I did to overcome it all to attain success, happiness and fulfillment. You'll learn the principles I applied to achieve what I desired in life and how you can instantly apply them in your life to get similar or greater results.

People have long come to me for advice and inspiration. They know I come from a place of hopelessness and that I overcame it. I've always loved being a listening ear and a guiding force and people say I'm good at it. They come back and thank me, sometimes years later, and tell me how much I changed their lives.

But one day, on the upward curve of a successful career and overall good life, I realized I was actually unhappy. I felt empty. When I got a promotion at work it felt like a demotion because, as I moved up in rank, I moved further from a direct connection with the people I served and that connection was my driving force. Eventually, I got injured at work (again) and a second procedure on my back took me away from my daily experience of helping others. While nursing my injury, I took an objective look at my situation and the prospects of my future. I realized that I was unhappy and unfulfilled unless I was helping, inspiring and empowering people. It gave my life purpose.

After searching within myself and asking the universe about my true life's purpose the answer finally came to me. Sacrifice all of myself. Sacrifice my pride, my dignity and anything else necessary to empower others to achieve greatness in their lives regardless of their past or current circumstances.

To do so, I'd have to give away the thing I held most dear to me— my story. To tell my story, I'd have to visit a level of vulnerability that I once promised myself I would never be subjected to again. I didn't want to hurt, appear weak or like less than a man. But I came to realize that my story didn't belong to me, it belonged to the world. I have no right to withhold it from its rightful owner.

I have so many reasons to be grateful. I have my own company; my wife has a non-profit organization and my children have careers in the arts. My ten-year-old son is an actor and dancer; my eldest daughter is a fifteen-year-old director and filmmaker who owns her own production company and my three-year-old daughter is always "performing." Although, I have achieved my American Dream, I used to try supporting my family on a four-figure annual income; but now—with serving others, empowering and uplifting humanity being the mission—we're building, what will soon be, a multi-million-dollar empire.

I decided to write this book because I believe that my story can change the world. I believe I can change the way individuals look at their lives. If a guy like me can overcome seemingly insurmountable odds and become successful, the notion that extraordinary achievement is impossible for you is only a tiny island surrounded by an ocean of possibility. Success and greatness are yours for the taking. Go get some—and Go Be Great!

CHAPTER 1 - NEVER GIVE ME AWAY

My mother considered having an abortion while she was pregnant with me. When it was too late for an abortion, she considered giving me up for adoption. She was only eighteen years old, the single mother of a two-year-old daughter and living with her own mother (Nana). My mother had no real income, no real stability in her life and no place of her own to call home. Nana told my mother early on during her pregnancy that I could not stay with her. Yet, when the doctors put me in her arms, my mother said she looked into my eyes and knew that she would never give me away.

When my mother and I left the hospital, she brought me to Nana's knowing I wasn't welcome. The roof was leaking so badly it rained inside the house. Even Nana was leaving. She and her boyfriend were going to stay at a hotel. As my mother stood in the street with me in her arms and holding my sister, Tiona's hand, she asked her mother, "Mom, can we come with you and sleep on the floor at the hotel?" Nana replied, "No, Tracey." and walked away.

So, we were homeless. My mother used to call it "moving and shaking." Reluctantly, but with no other choice, she had to ask my father if we could stay with him. My mother and father never lived in the same quarters for very long without things going sour. My father let us live with him but it didn't last long. I am not certain why, but if my mother tells the story, he kicked us out. My mother could be a handful. She was no saint, for sure. But, neither was my father. Speaking of our family situation, my father once told me "We were high every day, the whole situation was drug-induced. It wasn't no family."

So, we were homeless again. Moving and shaking. My mother looked into my eyes, just as she did when she said that she would never give me away—and she gave me away. My mother's aunt (my great aunt), "AV" as I call her—knew that my mother's life and living situation were unstable. AV had previously told my mother that if she ever needed help that she would take care of me until my mother got on her feet. Mom knew it was my only shot at a good life, so it was an easy decision—one of the hardest *easy* decisions she's ever had to make. She said she cried the entire way to AV's and the entire way back. Although I was born in Philadelphia I became a son of Lawnside. AV and Uncle Hal, her husband, loved and cared for me like I was their own son. Things were great for about a year and a half, but what happened next would change everything, for everyone.

On the Christmas of 1984, AV brought me to Philadelphia to see my mother, sister and other family members. We went to Nana's house, where everyone went for the holidays. Nana had a long dining room table and my mother tells the story of how I had these shoes on that were affixed to a metal bar because I was bowlegged. She says when I walked, I had to wobble like a penguin. She says I was on the table, at one end and she was at the other end and I wobbled my bowlegged self over to her swinging my legs one at a time as I twisted my hips: right hip, right foot, left hip, left foot. When I reached her, I gave a hug and I lay my head upon her shoulder. She held me tight, and, unable to fight back the tears, as she tells the story, she says that it was then that she knew she would never give me away again.

When AV came to get me, things escalated very quickly. Mom and AV (who I knew as "mom") were toe to toe. "Give me back my motherf— son and get the f— out of my face," my mother said. AV felt disrespected, enraged, and the scenario ended in a physical fight. I was AV's "second son," she raised me as her own, loved me as her own. She and Uncle Hal had grown very fond of me. But, on this day, I was Tracey's son and she would never give me away, again. After the altercation, the police were called and, when it was all said and done, I stayed with my biological mother.

CHAPTER 2 - MOVING AND SHAKING

We were together again mother, Tiona and I. Still with no place to call our own. We were on the streets, but we were on the streets together. We lived between our mom's sister's houses, her sisters' boyfriends' houses and her friends' houses for a while until mom found an ad in the paper for a room for $50 a week. The man renting the room in his house happened to be one of my mother's 10th grade teachers so he was happy to help our mother out. This was the best that she could do for her family at the time, because it was all that she could afford.

Mom had to pay someone $150 a week to watch Tiona and I while she went to work. She worked for the attorneys who were handling the infamous MOVE bombings in Philadelphia. She was doing well there. The attorneys liked her and she liked her job. Things were going seemingly well until she missed the bus on the way to work one day. She got fired after being late to open the office. With no job and no money, she couldn't pay someone to watch us. She had no way to afford her room and we ended up homeless, again. Moving and shaking.

We had a major breakthrough in the blessing department when a good friend of my mother's, who was known to us only as "Aunt Bunny," let us live with her. During our time there, my mother and father started revisiting the idea of living together.

After promising to break it off with a woman that he had been seeing, my father found himself in a sticky predicament. My mother unexpectedly showed up at his house and found that he was still with the woman. While my mother and father were arguing, the woman left and went outside to catch a cab. That's when the argument had reached a boiling point and my father, for the first time in their relationship, hit my mother. My mother says he beat her like she was a man. She said she was counting as he was hitting her seeing how many blows she would take before she passed out. She says she remembers counting to 12, but she never passed out.

She kept telling herself to fall to the ground but her knees wouldn't buckle so she couldn't fall. Eventually he just stopped hitting her and drug her outside.

My father tells a different story. He says he hit her only once that day. Although my father didn't go into details about the incident, he expressed remorse for hitting my mother. He said he never wanted to hit her but his father used to beat his mother, so he became accustomed to seeing a man beat a woman. My dad's father left his family when my dad was just fourteen years old.

My father told me after his mother died in 1986, he felt all alone. He felt his ability to love people as family went to the grave with her. He had been through lots of trauma in his life and then the only person that he felt loved him had lost her battle with cancer. A piece of him had died with his mother. At that point he felt he could never love anyone like they should be loved. His perceived inability to love was made apparent in his relationships. Eventually after his mother died, he'd lock himself in his house, close the blinds and just use crack-cocaine and alcohol all day long. The inability to deal with his mother's death sent him spiraling out of control. He lost everything. His job, his friends, his life as he knew it were all gone. Since he was jobless, and spent all his money on drugs and alcohol, he lost his house.

He let my mother, my sister and me move with him into his father's house in Darby, PA. Grand pop Al was a functioning alcoholic. He would have orange juice and vodka for breakfast and then leave for work. When he'd come home he'd get his drink, turn up his radio and play country music while watching TV until he passed out on the couch. I think Grand pop Al is where I got my affinity for country music.

Alfred Davis, my father's father used to encourage my Dad to beat my mother, right in front of Tiona and I, while she was pregnant with my sister, Sarina. "You better put that b— in her place," Grand pop would say, "teach her some damn respect!" And as Tiona and I would look on with absolute terror, Grand pop would watch my father punch my mother relentlessly while her back was to the wall, like a boxer who had his opponent against the ropes.

"Please Warren, don't do this in front of my kids," she'd beg. "Please." Just thinking about it, I have to fight back tears as I hear my mother plead for mercy. My father says he did it because she wouldn't give him the food stamps to go buy food for me and Tiona because she wanted to go buy crack and get high. My mother says my father was the one who wanted to use the food stamps to buy crack and get high. She also accused him of being with other women while he was with her and she believes her questioning him about that is what fueled some of his wrath and physical aggression.

We eventually left my grandfather's house. Yet again, we were homeless, moving and shaking. We ended up in New Jersey staying with my mother's sister, Aunt Tee. We eventually got our own place in the apartment complex at 601 Tatum Street, in Woodbury, NJ. And it wasn't long before my dad moved in with us. He brought the same behavior along with him. He was an alcoholic and he and my mother were both addicted to crack. There were many times that I heard him beating her and telling her to give him the food stamps. When she finally gave them up, he'd leave and we wouldn't see him for days, weeks, sometimes months. But he'd usually come back with flowers and an apology.

"Mommy, I hate my dad," I remember saying to her after seeing him beat her and leave the house. Her left eye was so swollen; tears were only flowing from her right eye. As she lay upon the floor, still trying to recover from the assault, she grabbed my hand and sunk her head in shame. "You don't hate your father, baby," she said, "you just hate what he docs." She always taught us to love, no matter what.

You Always Have a Choice

We should choose not to make excuses about our life's decisions. Our current life situation is exactly what it is because of our decisions. Regardless of our circumstances, our environment or whatever our perceived plight, we have choices. We have always had a choice, even when we thought we didn't—like my father, when his father encouraged him to abuse my mother. He had the choice to do what his father told him to do, or do what he felt was right. He decided that by abusing my mother, he would get more benefit from his father viewing him as a "man" and making his father happy than he would from sparing my mother the physical anguish.

Our choices have been what they have been because at the time that we made the decision, we weighed the benefits and we went with the decision that would be the most beneficial in that moment. We chose the one that would ensure us the most gratification, either instant gratification or future gratification. Oftentimes, we can make hasty decisions searching for instant gratification as opposed to making the decision that will ensure us long term gratification. How many times have we done that? How many decisions did we make in the moment, choosing the one that best suited us at that point? How many times have we regretted that decision years later? We must understand that life is so much more than just "this moment." We have to make our decisions based on our life's goals; based on what we want our outcome in that situation to be, not just what feels like it would be most beneficial in the moment. If we ask ourselves "How will this decision or that decision help me get closer to my goal or ensure I get my desired outcome," we'd make better choices, wouldn't we?

We must also hold ourselves accountable for our decisions, not deflect blame and responsibility. I hold myself accountable for all my life's choices. Many of them were not very good in my earlier years of life. Continuing to make excuses for our life's choices, rather than holding ourselves accountable, executing and making change hinders our growth. It'll force us to become stagnant, stuck in the past and ensure our continued detriment. Yes, some of our life's choices may contribute to our failures, but all of them will contribute to our success. So, make peace with your bad choices and make progress on your good ones.

CHAPTER 3 - THE WRITING ON THE WALL

I do not subscribe to "race." God created man in his image and likeness. God does not segregate. God is all inclusive because God is love. I love all people and all things that God has created. You may look at me or my skin color and you may judge me based on what you see, but I do not categorize or limit myself as far as race or "culture." Genesis 1:27 says "So God created man in his own image, in the image of God he created him; male and female he created them." That, I will not debate. But race… God didn't create race, God created man and God created woman. The concept of race is man-made. It segregates us and does the opposite to us what God intended. It breeds hate. If it is not Love, it is not of God and if it is not of God, I do not subscribe to it.

That said, for a while my family was the only family with a darker complexion living in the apartment complex at 601 Tatum St., in Woodbury, NJ. Most of the families living there had low incomes and we all had some similar struggles with family drug abuse, alcoholism, child neglect and so forth. But my family was the only family that was "different." We did not share the same skin complexion as the other families, so we were ostracized.

I remember once, we went to a party where some of our "friends" were celebrating one of the children's birthday. The young man whose birthday it was walked up to us and told us that his mom said "no n—are allowed at my party and you have to go."

Our birthday parties were always elaborate with decorations, delicious cake and ice cream and we always had fun. There were four of us and my mother threw a great party four times every year. Everyone wanted to be at our parties and we'd let them come, never discriminating. Our mother always taught us to love as a child of God. But we were "different," in more ways than one.

Because of our skin complexion, there were days when we would get chased home from school by groups of racist children. They would throw rocks at us, throw sticks and spit in our faces while calling us the "n" word. How six and seven year olds learned how to be so hateful is beyond me. I couldn't understand how this type of hatred was sewn so deeply into the fabric of that community. My mother still makes the joke today when she sees me: "Do you have your sticks in your pants and your rocks in your pockets?" We used to have to defend ourselves if we got attacked because we got tired of running.

Yet, sometimes I'd find other uses for those sticks and rocks such as the time Tiona, our friend Jay and I threw them at the school and Jay "accidentally" broke a window. We poked our heads inside the broken glass, careful to avoid cutting ourselves on the shards. There was nothing inside but desks and papers. It was some type of office. Tiona decided to climb inside and start throwing things out.

I stood on the outside, hysterically laughing, as tests and homework assignments came flying out of the window, then tape dispensers, Xerox paper, and even a random paperclip. I still laugh thinking about that single silver paperclip. I thought it was hilarious until I saw a police car coming toward us. "Cops!" I yelled to Tiona. I was trying to wait for her to get out but, when I heard the cop's car engine roar and the car came speeding in my direction, I panicked. I don't know what happened to Jay but I didn't care. I ran home and told my mother everything but, by the time she put her clothes and shoes on to go get Tiona, the police were pulling up with her in the back of the patrol car.

One of the only times I remember my mother beating us as a form of discipline was after that incident. My mother didn't believe in corporal punishment as a means of discipline for her children. But every now and again, she'd have to assert herself and beat us. But on that day, that beating was a joke! It barely hurt and we barely cried. We even laughed about it afterward— me, Tiona and Mom. I told her I fake cried to get her to stop and she just laughed. I don't think Mom could bring herself to hurt us. She did most of her disciplining through conversing with us and teaching us why we should not repeat specific behaviors.

"Spare the rod, spoil the child," didn't work in my case anyway. True, it kept me from being spoiled but it also made me angry and even more belligerently rebellious. I didn't like people hurting me and I wouldn't let anyone beat compliance into me. This frustrated a lot of adults throughout my life. Everyone, and I mean everyone wanted to beat me as a kid. Nana, aunts, uncles, dad, older cousins, everyone wanted to whoop my "yellow tail." If my mother was around, no one would beat her son. When she wasn't around, my yellow tail was red.

One evening my mom, Tiona and I were laying on my bed watching a movie when I saw smoke coming from behind the TV. Simultaneously, Tiona saw the electrical socket behind the bed spark and we all got off the bed. Then the lights went out in the apartment.

We went to Mr. Nestler's apartment and told him what happened. Mr. Nestler was the maintenance man. He went into the basement and restored the electricity to our apartment. We all left assuming everything was going to be fine. My mom, Sarina and Tiona went upstairs to visit Ms. Edy, Mom's friend. Dad went back to his room to watch TV. Ciara and I started playing hide and seek. I smelled smoke when I hid in the closet. I opened the closet and I saw smoke coming from my bedroom. "Dad, the house is on fire!" I yelled. He was already coming out of the room because he smelled the smoke too.

Dad called for my mom. I ran upstairs to Ms. Edy's apartment and told mom the house was on fire. She ran down the steps screaming, "Warren, Warren!" The mattress where Tiona, Mom and I were once laying was on fire. The sparks from the electrical socket set the bed ablaze. Trying to save the apartment, Mom opened the bedroom window and yelled to my dad to help throw the bed out of the window.

My father was already running from the kitchen, equipped with the cover to the barbecue grill, which he had "filled" with water, not realizing the cover had holes (usually to allow smoke to escape.) So, when he ran back to the room and threw the water onto the fire, there was barely any water to throw. Most of the water ended up on the floor from the kitchen to the bedroom as it spilled right out of the ventilation holes before he got to the bedroom. The little bit of water that he did throw onto the fire only enraged it.

The water made the fire spread rapidly and uncontrollably. We battled the flames for a moment, but we quickly came to grips with the harsh reality that we had lost the battle with the now raging inferno and we had to abandon our extinguishing efforts. I remember sobbing uncontrollably as I watched our belongings burn—our toys, our clothes, our stuffed animals. I ran out of my bedroom in shock. It was as if things were moving in slow motion as I looked back over my shoulder. I could taste the smoke as it filled my lungs. I could hear the crackling and popping of the wood as it burned. I could feel the intense heat and see the paint bubbling on the walls.

There is nothing like watching helplessly as your family loses everything, especially when you come from "nothing". I remember my father asking my mother "What are we going to do?" In a moment like that our family could only do what our family always did— move and shake.

After the fire, we moved back into the apartment. Even though the walls were charred, a few windows were busted out and everything we owned was basically destroyed, we lived there for about two months. All five of us; mom, myself and my three sisters slept on one single mattress on the living room floor. I don't know where my father was during that time. The carpet was still wet from all the water the fire department used to put out the fire. Eventually, Mom cleaned the smoke and soot off the walls in her bedroom and we moved the mattress in there.

There was no electricity. We ran an extension cord out the kitchen window, down into the basement window of the apartment building, to the plug behind the washing machine to get power. We shared one lamp connected to an extension cord to illuminate the entire apartment. When it was time to cook, the lamp was in the kitchen. When it was time to eat, the lamp was in the dining room and when it was time to take baths we all took one together with the lamp in the bathroom. Somehow through it all, my mother always kept our spirits high and we never saw our situation as troubling. We never felt like things were bad. We just did what we had to do to get by. Poverty being all we knew; we didn't even know we were poor. We did not know that we were suffering as a family. This was normal living for us.

Funny thing, the brain. It's funny how once a poverty mindset sinks in, and you accept poverty as your reality, you don't even realize you're poor. You just accept that way of living, thinking and doing things. Some don't even attempt to fathom anything better than what they have in their lives. In this poverty mindset, they accept their world the way it is and never try to make a greater life for themselves. I was once interviewed by Joe Pardo on the "Dreamers Podcast" and he asked me what were some of the dreams I had as a kid. He was surprised when I told him that I didn't have any dreams. I mean sure, I wanted to be a police officer since I was very young, but I never truly thought I'd become one. I never dreamed about it, I never saw myself as an adult achieving that goal because I didn't live my life like someone who was trying to become a police officer. I didn't have the life of a kid who could become that. I don't make a lot of promises or guarantees, but I guarantee you, if you adopt a poverty mindset, you will experience the plight of poverty. One more guarantee that I will make is this: you can change your mindset. Change your mindset, change your life.

Mother had been working on getting us into another apartment in the complex. Meanwhile, we were going to school with our clothes smelling like either we just barbequed our breakfast or we just escaped a burning building. We had gotten accustomed to the smell and, eventually, I didn't even notice it. But my classmates did. They didn't miss an opportunity to draw attention to it. We just couldn't seem to wash the smell out of our belongings. We knew we just had to hold on until we got our next apartment.

Then, one day, our apartment finally came through. We were moving from 6A into 5A, and it was renovated! It was only the next building over but it was like a new chapter in our lives. Like the Phoenix we rose from the ashes. Okay, maybe not quite like the Phoenix—maybe more like an eagle, pigeon or duck—but we rose up. Moving to a normal apartment was such a big deal for us after living in what we used to call Freddy Krueger's house. We watched the Freddy Krueger poster, that was above the bed in our old room, go up in flames the day apt. 6A caught fire. That day felt like a scene out of the movie *"Nightmare on Elm Street."*

We never had anything to call our own until Apt. 6A, and that was a smokehouse in more ways than one. So, we were ecstatic about the new apartment. But then there's always Murphy's Law. And on October 28, 1983 a small caveat was added to Murphy's Law: Anything that can go wrong, will go wrong; and if Travis Wolfe is involved, you can bet it will. Adults in my family, except my mom and dad always told me I was a troublemaker, so that's what I became. Knowing that the people in that neighborhood didn't like my family because we were darker-skinned, I should have behaved differently. But I ignored the writing on the wall. In fact, one of the reasons we got evicted was because of the writing on the wall, but not proverbial kind.

I was into a lot of silly childhood mischief with the other kids from the neighborhood. And, although we played together, it was no secret that the people of that neighborhood didn't want me and my family there. It didn't help that I sometimes fit right into *their* stereotypes of darker-skinned people by getting into trouble. They did everything they could to get rid of us. And between six and eight years old, unbeknownst to me, I was helping them. They often made comments to us letting us know we weren't wanted there and they were going to "get you ni—s out of here!" I still didn't see the writing on the wall.

My mother and I had to go to court because of some mischief I was involved in. My school principal gave us a ride home from court. My mother decided to keep me home from school for the rest of the day. Later that afternoon, a police officer came to our apartment and told my mother that I had broken a window in the neighborhood after school. Befuddled, my mother said to the officer, "Sir, how could that be when my son has been home with me all day?"

The people in that Woodbury/ West Deptford neighborhood would tell the police I did things that I didn't do because they wanted us out of their neighborhood. The apartment management was looking to evict us. If windows got broken, property got vandalized, something got stolen, they blamed me, which was unnecessary since I got into more than enough trouble on my own.

I was arrested at the age of seven and my "partner in crime," Steven, was also arrested. We were walking to school one morning and one or both of us had the genius idea to cut through the yards to get to school faster. As we jumped fences and trampled flower beds, we came upon a shed. The shed was custom built, red-painted wood with a black, shingled roof. This shed was massive and surely, inside there would be something of sizable awesomeness for us to play with. So, Steven and I went in.

In the shed were two massive snow mobiles. Though the leaves on the ground were not the suggested terrain for snowmobiles, we were determined to ride them. We found the nearest gas can and commenced to filling up the gas tanks on the snowmobiles. Unbeknownst to us, there was oil in the gas can and not gas. We were caught red handed, holding the red gas can, as the door of the shed swung open. An angry middle aged man was in the doorway. "What the hell you bastards doing?!" he shouted. He grabbed us by the wrists, pulled us off his snowmobiles and called the police.

When the police came, they took us to the station and I was placed in a cell, alone. Steven was sitting on a bench. I'm pretty sure, now, that it was not proper protocol to put a 7-year-old in a cell but, nevertheless, I believed that I was supposed to end up "dead or in jail just like my father." So, in my mind, I was right where I belonged. It had no major effect on me. In fact, the effect was so little, I didn't even tell my mother until years later, she says. To this day, she still brings up the fact that I should have told her when it happened.

With every mischievous act, every broken window, every visit from the police to the apartments on the account of me, I gave management at the apartment complex more fuel for their fiery hate-filled agenda until they had just enough ammunition to get us kicked out of our apartment. I used a pipe to damage a washing machine and hit the gas meters in the basement of the apartment building and wrote on the wall of the building with crayon. Oh, I also defended myself from racist kids who attacked us at the behest of their parents. The judge called it "fighting with the neighbors." Hate-filled agenda or not, admittedly, I was causing some problems there. The worst thing was, I did all this between the ages of six and eight years old. After we had finally found a place to call home, one that looked like a home and felt like home, I managed to get us evicted. If only I had seen the writing on the wall. And I don't mean the message that read "*F— you Mom. Love, Travis.*"

The other kids were writing all kinds of profanity and stupidity on the wall but I was always the guy who had to do it bigger and better than everyone else. I knew I could top them all by going where no one would dare. Someone already wrote "F— You." So, I needed to "one up" them. I took my crayon to the tan concrete wall and I wrote out what would essentially spell out my family's detriment: F— you Mom. Love, Travis. I wanted to solidify my position as the coolest kid in town. I loved my mom more than anything in the world, but it wasn't about her, it was about me being the man. Everyone knew I was the kid that did things that everyone else was too afraid to do. I had to live up to that. I didn't even think about how it would make my mother feel when she saw it. To this day, even after I tell her I did it, she still tells me I didn't do it. I don't know if it hurts her that much or if she just truly believed me when I originally lied and said I didn't do it.

I was only seven years old. I didn't understand why my behavior was detrimental, and no one ever explained it to me. But, I make no excuses. I made those choices and I put my family in a terrible situation because of those choices. My mother didn't teach us to hate but only to love everyone as God loves us. Not knowing or understanding hate, I didn't understand the correlation between people's hatred for us and my actions and the detriment it would cause down the line. Had I understood, maybe my actions would have been different, maybe not. But, I take full responsibility for my actions. My parents taught me better; I knew the difference between right and wrong. I just didn't know that my wrongs would make things so bad for my family. For a long time, I struggled with the pain of knowing that it was me that ruined the only stable living situation my family ever had. Mom never blames me. She won't place the blame on me nor will she allow me to place the blame on myself. But I know what I did. I didn't see the writing on the wall, until I wrote it myself. Unfortunately for us, what I wrote spelled out EVICTION.

CHAPTER 4 - OFFICER STEVE

It was 1992 and I had just gotten my family evicted from our apartment in Woodbury, NJ. My mother, my three sisters, Tiona, Sarina, Ciara and I were living in the Ambler Motel in the nearby town of Brooklawn. Every day a police officer (known to us as "Officer Steve") would come to the Ambler Motel where we lived and check on our family. He'd bring us candy, donuts or other snacks from the food establishments along US 130. He'd sometimes even go grocery shopping for us to make sure we had the essentials until our mom came back home. He'd knock on our door with that "Who da hell knockin' on my door like they da PO-LICE!" knock. He'd come inside, and with his hands on his waist, he'd look around. Then, he'd ask us, "Where's your mom?" He knew like we knew she was out getting high.

For the most part mom was usually home with us but there were many times when she wasn't or she was but she'd be getting high. When she was home getting high, we would mess with her. We knew she just wanted to be left alone and didn't want us to see her in that state. She'd lock herself in the motel bathroom and we knew, once we smelled that indescribable yet unmistakable scent of burnt crack, we could get away with anything. I'd knock on the door like I was the PO-LICE. "Mom, can I have some money to go to the store?"

I could sense her frustration as she threw the glass crack pipe down on the porcelain bathroom sink and searched for enough money for all four of us to leave her alone for a couple of hours. It was always an easy $20. "Mom, can we ride our bikes?" "Mom, can we go to the park?" "Mom, Mom, Mom, MOM?!" We got everything we wanted when she was getting high. We'd just hit her with a barrage of questions in rapid succession because she couldn't handle the pressure in that state.

Sometimes, instead of just giving in, she'd pack up and sneak out of the bathroom and we wouldn't know until we heard the front door close. By the time we got to the door and opened it, she was gone. If we caught her before she vanished, we'd corner her and try to keep her from leaving. "Mom, don't lea…"

"Don't call me Mom, call me Bambi," she'd scold. Whenever she was upset with us, she'd tell us to call her Bambi. Before she left us alone, she'd put on Michael Jackson's Moonwalker or Bambi. Those were my favorite movies growing up. The movie Bambi would become symbolic for me as figuratively, I lost my mother growing up.

Officer Steve would encourage our mother to get herself clean so that she could take care of us properly and he'd encourage us to stick together. He said if we just stuck together and loved each other, everything would be alright. He always told me I was the man of the house and had to look after and protect my sisters.

Jimmy and Chrissy lived two doors down from us. Jimmy was ten and Chrissy was thirteen; they were Tiona's friends. Jimmy and Chrissy's mother would buy them a carton of cigarettes that they'd all smoke together. My mother and father smoked cigarettes so I was used to seeing that but seeing a parent smoke with their children, that was unbelievable to me. One day, for some reason, Tiona and I got a cigarette from them. We took our cigarette and snuck around to the side of the motel and lit that sucker up. I took a drag and damn near choked to death. Instantly, I got bronchitis. I got asthma. I got influenza. I felt like I had small shards of glass in my lungs.

When Tiona and I walked from around the side of the motel, we saw Officer Steve. He must've been able to smell the cigarette smoke emanating from us.
"And just what are you two doing?" he asked.

"Nothing," I replied while avoiding making eye contact.

"Where's your mom and do I need to go tell her what you're doing?"

"We ain't doin' nothin', Officer Steve," I protested.

He gave me that stern look that a father gives you when you messed up. I felt like he was staring into my soul. I could feel him staring at me long after he drove away. When Officer Steve came back later that afternoon he had a bag full of candies for us, among them, candy cigarettes.

People would look at my sisters and I and call us the "n" word as they spat on us. Other kids would chase us home from school slinging rocks, sticks and slurs at us. Although our community ostracized us, Officer Steve, who did not look like us, showed us love and compassion like nothing we had ever experienced from anyone outside of our family. What this man showed us was the unconditional love of God that flows through all creation. Officer Steve saw us for who we were regardless of our circumstances or our perceived differences.

One day at the motel, my mother's sisters, Aunt Dee and Aunt Kissy, were arguing in our room about something. To this day I don't know what the argument was about, but it was heated. My mother was between them. Aunt Kissy was pointing her finger around the left side of my mother's head, putting it in Aunt Dee's face, and Aunt Dee was pointing her finger around the right side of my mother's head, putting it in Aunt Kissy's face. Every expletive imaginable came off the lips of either one of my aunts. My mother kept pushing them away from each other but they kept charging one another.

Before I knew it, BOOM! I didn't even see it happen, I don't think anyone did. All I know is there was arguing then scuffling and then Aunt Kissy ran out of the house, holding her face, screaming "You stabbed me in my f— face b—!"

My mother and sisters ran after aunt Kissy. Stunned, I looked at my Aunt Dee. The room was silent except for her deep, rapid breaths. She wouldn't even look at me. She just started pacing back and forth. I ran out to catch up to everyone else. As I exited the motel room, there was so much blood. There was a trail of blood from our room to the grass where Aunt Kissy was now slowly walking with my mother beside her trying to hold her up. As I followed behind them, careful not to step in her blood with my bare feet, Aunt Kissy collapsed beneath my favorite tree. Her blood colored the green grass red.

I remember standing over her, wondering how it all happened so fast and why I wasn't able to stop it (most likely because I'm not a ninja.) Aunt Dee didn't mean to do this, did she? Is Aunt Kissy going to die? I asked myself a thousand questions in that moment. Where is Officer Steve? I don't remember whether he came that day. I remember wishing he was there, so maybe he didn't come. What did come to me was what he told me about protecting my sisters. I immediately began to look for them.

I saw Ciara run behind the motel, crying. Sarina, Tiona and I followed behind her. We all huddled together to comfort one another. If there was one thing we knew how to do, we knew how to stick together through any and every situation. We had been exposed to a lot of things we shouldn't have at that age. The youngest of us, five, and the eldest of us, ten. But, this moment was like none other for Ciara because of the people involved. Aunt Dee was Ciara's biological mother.

Aunt Dee was very young and her living situation was unstable when she had Ciara so she was not able to care for Ciara as well as she would have liked. So, my mother, already having three children of her own, took Ciara in from the time she was just six months old and raised her as her own. So, although biologically, Ciara is our cousin, she is also our sister.

I can't imagine the emotion Ciara was feeling after watching her biological mother stab her own sister. Ciara was only six years old when she witnessed that stabbing. It was possible she might not see her biological mother for a long time or for life because of it. I just hugged her and let her know everything was going to be alright. That memory for me fades out like the final scene of a movie; I don't remember ever letting her go.

We got evicted not long after that. Officer Steve started checking on us more frequently and the increased police presence after "The Sister Incident", as my siblings and I call it, brought attention to the prostitution ring that was operating in the motel. So, the motel management got rid of us.

I remember sitting outside amongst our things, daydreaming. We could not afford a moving truck. We were just sitting there, waiting for someone to help us move all our belongings back to Philadelphia. We could not be in the property, so we just sat outside with our large, black, plastic trash bags, our boxes and other miscellaneous items scattered about. Seeing my little sisters sharing a bag of my soiled laundry as a pillow while they slept outside on the grass, absolutely crushed me. As the night grew closer, I was more hopeful, praying that someone would come to help us. But no one came.

I could hear the crickets chirping as I lay on my back watching the night sky. A plane flew overhead, probably from Philly International Airport across the river. Trying to escape my hellish reality, I imagined myself in that plane. I could see the calm waters of the Delaware River from my window seat. The bright lights of the city illuminated the ground beneath me. I could see us, my family, lying in the grass below, just outside the motel. And me, looking up at the plane I was riding in, wishing I was truly there and wasn't just imagining it. We gave up hope of someone coming to rescue us from our situation and slept there, huddled together, chest-to-back, trying to keep one another warm by sharing body heat. The fall night was cold, the grass was wet and though together, we were the loneliest we had ever been.

As the single mother of four, having no hope to hold on to, having no light at the end of the proverbial tunnel, what would you tell your children in this situation? My mother was so strong. She didn't shed a tear. Her attitude was positive and her words were encouraging because she knew it was the only thing that could keep us from falling apart. Even in her addiction, she was so strong.

Ironically, as detached as she was from us physically throughout our lives, she was always the glue that held us all together.

We took turns keeping watch. When it was my turn, I sobbed uncontrollably as I blamed myself. If I didn't get us evicted from our apartment at 601 Tatum Street, we would still have a place to live, Aunt Kissy never would have gotten stabbed and Aunt Dee wouldn't be in prison.

The Company You Keep

One major, not-so-secret "secret to success" is being deliberate about the company you keep. Actively search for role models and mentors who have integrity and who strive for high ideals. If you spend a lot of time around complainers, liars, and those with a negative mindset, you will become as they are. When you surround yourself with people who possess these negative qualities, whether you intentionally attempt to take on these characteristics or not, you will unconsciously adopt similar traits and ambitions. Now, if you're thinking, "No, not me, I don't let anyone influence me, I have total control over what I do, what I want and who I become" you're not alone. I once thought that way, too. But, as the great Jim Rohn puts it, "You are the average of the five people you spend the most time with." If you have some characteristics that you don't necessarily prefer, evaluate the company you keep.

The great thing about this principle is, if you associate with those who value honor, integrity, generosity, philanthropy and love —those who give of themselves, help others and chase total life fulfillment every waking moment—you will adopt their attitudes, behaviors and beliefs. Whose behaviors and beliefs would you want to adopt?

Who are some role models of yours, people you look up to, or aspire to be like?

In the chart, below, place the names of the 5 people you spend the most time with. Next to their name, place traits or qualities that they possess that you also possess. Alternatively, if you have trouble finding a quality that you both share, you can choose to write things that they do or like to do that you also do or like to do. Challenge yourself to find a common trait or quality.

Names of the five people you spend the most time with	List character traits or qualities that you both share

In the chart, below, place the names of the 5 people you would like to spend time with; a role model or someone you admire who you aspire to be like/look up to. Next to their name, list qualities that they have that you do not currently possess but desire to acquire. Alternatively, list things that they do that you desire to do, as well.

Names of five people you admire and would like to spend time with	List a character trait or quality this person has that you desire

If you have honestly filled in the charts above, you should notice that you are very comparable to the people you spend the most time with. Naturally, wanting to be comfortable, we befriend individuals that share similar traits, likes, dislikes, behaviors and pastimes as our own. If you continue to spend the majority of your time with these same individuals, you will continue to be the average of those 5 individuals. Which one of them can push you to new heights of greatness in your life? Which of them has a burning desire for greatness and is chasing it? Which of them motivate and inspire you to be better than you are. Who encourages you when you don't believe in yourself?

If you can find anyone in your group who does those things, keep close to them and spend less time with the others that don't. If you find that you're the smartest, most driven and most positive person in your group, it's time for you to find a new group. You need to surround yourself with individuals who are successful or who want to attain success. Seek people who are smart, driven and positive who will push you to get outside of your comfort zone. You will have no choice but to get to that next level.

Many of us enjoy the company of people whom live check to check, whom are jobless or barely living as middle-class. In such circles, we don't speak about financial growth, investing, starting businesses, mutual funds, stocks, blessing others, or the power of the laws of attraction or compensation. We won't normally hear names like Earl Nightingale, Andrew Carnegie, Napoleon Hill, Les Brown, Bob Proctor, Zig Ziglar, Dr. Eric Thomas, Dr. John C. Maxwell or Tony Robbins; nor do we hear of their books that uplift and inspire. Instead, we speak about being poor, not being able to wait until our next check comes in, what celebrity is doing what, how much we hate our jobs, bosses, lives, wives, husbands and situations.

Change your associations. Dare to get yourself around individuals who do speak only about positive things; people who read those books and practice the not-so-secret secrets to success 24/7/365. Desire to be greater than you are today. If you surround yourself with people who are successful—who think, dream and speak only about success—that you will become. For, what your focus is upon, that you will attract and become.

CHAPTER 5 - NEVER GIVE ME AWAY, PT. 2

We were again without a place to call our own. Moving and shaking. When we got to Nana's, I was just happy to be surrounded by walls again. Everyone loved Nana's house because, when you were there, you knew you'd likely see some family members who you didn't get to see often. We could see Aunt Tee's kids, who were our favorite cousins, or we could see our great aunts and uncles from Virginia who were always so nice to us. It was also a safe haven. To this day people in the family go there when they have nowhere else to go. But for some reason, even though we had nowhere else to go, we were not welcome to come there to live. This would become particularly apparent this day.

Not long after we got to Nana's, Mom disappeared. Having no home and no hope, she did the thing she knew best to do in situations that were tough for her to cope with—she got high. The difference between her leaving us at Nana's this time, and any other time before, is this would be the last time she walked out that door as the mother of four children.

When mom came back to Nana's house, she didn't hear us. Nana had a wind chime hanging on her vestibule door so, when the door opened, everyone knew there was a visitor. All the kids would run to the door to see who was visiting. But when Mom walked in, no one came running. No one ran up and hugged her, happy to see her. No one screamed "MOMMY!" In fact, Nana and Aunt Tee didn't even say anything to her. They wouldn't even make eye contact with her. They just acted as if she wasn't there. Aunt Tee huddled her kids all together in the kitchen and just left Mom standing there, befuddled. Mom said at that moment it hit her—she knew our own family had given us away. Can you imagine leaving out the door the mother of four children and later walking back in and having none? My mother said she cried pretty much nonstop for three days. Her own family placed her children in the foster care system.

REVIEW BOARD
RECOMMENDATION TO JUDGE
Superior Court – Family Division
(The Child Placement Review Act-N.J.S.A. 30:4C-50 et seq.)

INSTRUCTIONS
1. Type an original and send to judge
2. Send copy to DYFS, parents / legal guardian and appropriate interested parties
3. Make copy for CPR file

CHILD	DATE OF BIRTH	AGE	COUNTY	CPR DOCKET #
TRAVIS WOLFE	10/28/83	9	GLOUCESTER	FC-08-30-93-A

DYFS CASE MANAGER NAME	DYFS SUPERVISOR NAME	DYFS CASE NO
Brenda Craig	Roberta Rubinstein	KC-369806-12

DATE OF ORIGINAL PLACEMENT	DATE OF THIS PLACEMENT (if different from ORIGINAL)	REVIEW DATE: October 27, 1992
9/14/92		

REVIEW TYPE		DATE OF CURRENT ASSESSMENT
XX 45-Day Initial ___DYFS Goal Change ___New Placement Plan ___Return Home ___At Home ___12 Month ___Special		9/28/92

AUTHORITY FOR PLACEMENT	DYFS PLACEMENT TYPE (Short term plan)	DYFS LONG-TERM GOAL
XX Voluntary (signed)	___ Group Care Home	Family Reunification with:
___ Court Ordered	___ Institution (Med/Rehab/Psych)	XX Parent(s)/Guardian
___ Other (explain)	___ Residential Facility (Educ/Treatment)	___ Relative (Specify Relationship below)
	XX Foster Home	
	___ Other (explain)	___ Long-Term Foster Care
		___ Other (Specify)

___ Independent Living (Individual stabilization)
___ Institutionalization
Adoption:
___ By Foster parent(s)
___ Selected home
___ Undetermined

Is this placement appropriate?
Review Board: XX Yes ___ No

1. Date DYFS long-term goal to be achieved (Permanent Living Arrangement): Nov. 1993
2. Date Satisfies Review Board: XX Yes ___ No
3. Review Board permanent living arrangement date: _____

BOARD FINDINGS (To be used in combination with BOARD RECOMMENDATIONS below):

___ A. Continued placement of the child outside of the home is not in the child's best interest and the child should be returned home within two (2) weeks and the division or designated agency, as appropriate, shall provide reasonable and available services which are necessary to implement the return home.

XX B. Continued placement outside of the home is in the child's best interest on a temporary basis until the long-term goal is achieved.

___ C. Continued placement outside of the home on a temporary basis is in the child's best interest, but there is not sufficient information for the board to make a recommendation, therefore, the board requests the court to order the division or designated agency, as appropriate, to provide the needed information within two (2) weeks of the court order.

BOARD RECOMMENDATIONS

___ A. Sufficient information to be provided within two (2) weeks (date)_____
___ B. Placement plan to be modified within thirty (30) days (date)_____
___ C. New plan to be reviewed within thirty (30) days (Include new goal)

___ D. Summary Hearing
___ E. Show Cause Hearing
___ F. CASA be assigned
XX G. Red Flag - special conditions exist
___ H. Other _____

1) DYFS / designated agency Placement Plan Satisfies CPR (N.J.S.A. 30:4C-52) Legal criteria	2) DYFS / designated agency Placement Plan Satisfies Review Board	3) Necessary steps have been taken by DYFS / designated agency to implement the plan	4) Is it necessary for placement to continue? Review Board:
XX Yes ___ No	XX Yes ___ No	XX Yes ___ No	XX Yes ___ No

BOARD RECOMMENDATIONS EXPLANATION Child has been voluntarily placed in care. Mother, Tracy Wolfe, has neglected child. Mother's admitted addiction to drugs incapacitates her for nurturance of her children. Travis, for reasons of severe neglect is expected to need comprehensive medical, social, personal and emotional evaluation and subsequent treatment may be indicated.

CASE IS RED FLAGGED.

CHAIRPERSON CHILD PLACEMENT REVIEW BOARD (Signature)	DATE SIGNED
Earl Hinton, Chairperson Board No. 1	11/9/92

Administrative Office of the Courts

As if being given away by my mother shortly after I was born wasn't enough, I had been given away, again. This time, to people who weren't even family. I guess it was too much for anyone in the family to care for us. Aunt Tee loaded us up in the car and drove away from Nana's. The mood during the ride was somber. I think we were all trying to wrap our minds around what was going on. I don't think we fully understood the gravity of what was happening. Once we arrived at the Division of Youth and Family Services (DYFS) building in West Deptford, NJ it hit me. Life as we knew it was coming to an end. The worst part of it wasn't the unknown, going to live with strangers. The worst part was feeling like we were going to live with strangers because no one in our family loved us enough to take care of us. It was a feeling of betrayal, mixed with hatred mixed with love, mixed with fear. Of course, as they split my sisters and I up, we cried and screamed and held on tightly to one another as they peeled us apart. Ciara and Sarina went in one home and Tiona and I in another.

My first foster parent was a woman by the name of Mrs. Brice, who lived in Paulsboro, NJ. Mrs. Brice was a burly, middle-aged woman who had zero tolerance for misbehaved children. You misbehaved, you got beat and you didn't eat. Mrs. Brice had a large dog. She kept large bags of dog food in the basement and the foster children were tasked with feeding the dog. When she didn't feed me I'd go to go into the basement with the dog and eat dog food from the bag or from the dog's bowl.

I was absolutely no angel but I didn't deserve the physical abuse I got from Mrs. Brice. When I saw her coming with the board or the belt, I used to wish to God that I could slip into a coma so I wouldn't feel it. By that time, I knew the difference between beatings for the sake of discipline and beating for the sake of beating. This was abuse. By today's standards, Mrs. Brice would have been arrested for the things she did to me. Being a victim of racism growing up, I sometimes thought she hated me because of my skin color, but she absolutely loved my sister, Tiona and the other foster child, Kimmy, who was of Korean and Haitian descent.

Aunt Tee was the contact person from our family for the courts in New Jersey overseeing the placement of the Wolfe Children. One day, the court sent a letter to my Aunt Tee explaining to her the rules of the court for visitation. The paperwork had the addresses of the homes where my sisters and I were staying and, one day, Aunt Tee brought my mother to see us unexpectedly. Maybe Aunt Tee had guilt for her role in placing us into the foster care system. Maybe she just thought she was making things right by bringing my mother to see us where we lived. Regardless, the courts called this action 'premature reunification.' They frowned upon premature reunification because it could disrupt the stability of the child. They were correct.

When my mother asked me how things were going there with Mrs. Brice, I told her that Mrs. Brice was beating me often. Mom had some choice words for Mrs. Brice, who wasn't fazed the least bit. Mom may have even tried to fight her, I don't remember those details too well. Mrs. Brice was husky, and even as an older woman of 58 years, she had absolutely no fear of some young drug-addict raving about not beating her child. After Mom left that day, I got worse. I took my do-what-I-want attitude to an entirely different level! In my mind, Mrs. Brice couldn't touch me now because my Mom will come back in here and... Mrs. Brice showed me immediately that I had the wrong idea. All the anger she didn't take out on my mom, she took out on me. I got my butt whooped more than ever. Maybe it was because I was acting out more or maybe it was because Mrs. Brice was mad at my mother. Or, maybe it was a combination of both. Either way, I couldn't bear it any longer.

I told Tiona I couldn't take it anymore and I was running away. We cried together but she understood that I had to go. I ran away from Mrs. Brice's house that day. By nightfall, I was only about 30 yards from the house. The house was on a lot of land that was surrounded by trees and wooded area. I was afraid to get lost, so I went back home and, as you can imagine, Mrs. Brice beat me when I got there. Later that evening, my caseworker came and took me from that home to another. Apparently, Ms. Brice couldn't take it anymore either.

I was so traumatized by then, after everything I had gone through in life, I don't remember much of anything about the next foster home that I went to except for my foster mother's name, Florence Fraction. She was an older woman, kind of like a grandmother. The rest is all a blur.

During the six months we spent in foster care, we visited our siblings at the office pretty consistently. My mother was supposed to be there many times, but she usually didn't make it. I don't ever remember a time she came so see us at the office during actual visiting days. In fact, when she came to Mrs. Brice's house was likely the only time I had seen her during the entire six months. I remember getting really excited around her birthday, thinking she'd finally show up for visitation at the office this time. We had a cake there and everything. We sat there, forever, awaiting her arrival. Our caseworker, Brenda Craig said "Alright y'all, 30 more minutes and I have to get y'all home."

Just as the 30 minutes was up, the door popped open. I turned, happy as I could be. I was ready to greet my mother with a big hug and a smile, but Mrs. Craig walked in. "Time to go guys, I'm sorry, Tracey isn't coming." She never came. We were devastated. Well, not Tiona. Tiona had been disappointed by my mother many more times than I had. She was used to it. Whenever she was about to feel pain, "F— it" was her defense. I still remember the warmth of those tears as they streamed down my face. This seemingly inescapable feeling of abandonment plagued my world. This was supposed to be a great time. Instead, it was just more disappointment, just as before. And they wondered why I had "issues."

I hated therapy. In therapy, they made me write apology letters to family, and to random strangers, for stuff that my family told them that I had done. I was barely eight years old. I felt betrayed by my family. And by family, I meant Aunt Tee. She told these DYFS people too much about me. Though her intentions were to help me, at that time it only made me feel betrayed. It's her fault I'm here and now she's telling these strangers all my business, I thought to myself. And then this woman I don't even know is making me feel like something is wrong with me. Maybe there was something wrong with me. Per the recommendation to the Judge from the Review Board: "Tracey Wolfe has neglected children. Mother's admitted addiction to drugs incapacitates her for nurturance of her children. Travis, for reasons of severe neglect, is expected to need a comprehensive medical, social, personal and emotional evaluation and subsequent treatment may be indicated." Someone, obviously thought something was wrong with me.

I was deliberately resistant and none of that therapy worked. I wouldn't allow it to. I didn't like the feeling of being manipulated. I could feel them trying to bait me into saying certain things or doing certain things and I didn't like it. I did not like people trying to get the answers out of me that they wanted; I wanted to give them the answers that I wanted them to have. I hated the feeling of some man or some woman sitting in front of me acting like they know me when they've never met me before, not realizing they've seen hundreds or thousands of kids like me before. I detested the feeling of someone looking at me and judging me. I'm not just some badass kid by choice. Things have happened to me that may be some of the cause to why I am the way I am. Let's talk about that! But with those glaring eyes, I could see them looking at me, judging me, talking to me with this generalized tone like I'm just one of their normal patients. I wanted to be treated as an individual. I'm Travis Wolfe, not the kid you saw earlier today or last week.

NOTICE of
CHILD PLACEMENT REVIEW
BOARD MEETING
Superior Court–Family Division
(The Child Placement Review Act-N J S A 30:4C-50 et seq)

INSTRUCTIONS

1. Prepare an original and file copy.
2. Prepare appropriate number of copies for interested parties unless waived by the court.
3. Enclose CPR Brochure with this notice.

CHILD	DATE OF BIRTH	AGE	COUNTY	CPR DOCKET #
Travis Wolfe	10/28/83	9	Gloucester	FC-08-30-93A

The Child Placement Review Board is an arm of the Superior Court – Family Division. The Board is a group of five citizens who review, at least once a year, the plans for all children who are placed outside their homes by the Division of Youth and Family Services (DYFS). Following the review, the Board makes one of the following recommendations to the judge who will then enter the final order:

A. Return the child to his / her parents or legal guardian within two (2) weeks;

B. Continue placement of the child out of the home in accordance with the DYFS plan until goal is accomplished;

C. Continue placement of the child out of the home on a temporary basis until further information is submitted by DYFS.

Please attend the Board meeting on the date and time listed below.

The Board welcomes any other information, written or oral, which will help in making a recommendation.

Direct your questions or other information concerning the review to the Board at the address or telephone number shown below.

REVIEW DATE	REVIEW TIME	REVIEW LOCATION
Tuesday October 27, 1992	8:00 p.m.	Justice Complex, Jury Assembly Room, Second Floor (Main Entrance) Hunter & Euclid Sts., Woodbury, NJ

CHILD PLACEMENT REVIEW BOARD COORDINATOR'S NAME	(AREA CODE) TELEPHONE NUMBER
L. Witasick	609-853-3727

CHILD PLACEMENT REVIEW BOARD MAILING ADDRESS	CPR BOARD #
Court House Annex, N.Broad & Hunter, P.O. Box 638, Woodbury, New Jersey 08096	1

COPIES TO:

☐ Child ☒ Mother ☐ Father ☐ Attorney

☐ Legal Guardian ☒ DYFS ☒ Foster Parent(s) ☐ Non-Custodial Parent

☒ Other __Maternal Grandmother__
✓Maternal Aunt

FAMILY DIVISION CASE MANAGER	DATE OF NOTICE
A.G.C.	October 13, 1992

Administrative Office of the Courts   CP0007 (Rev 10/90)

34

Seek To Attain the Counsel of Wise Men

Sometimes in our lives we come to a place where limited experience presents a challenge for us. We can get to a place where we do not know what is best for us in a particular situation. In those times, you may want to consider letting someone else show you or tell you what's the best way to proceed based on their life's experiences. Admitting to ourselves that sometimes we just don't have the wisdom to make the best decisions in certain situations is critical. Too often, without seeking the counsel of wiser men/women, we hastily make the decision we perceive is best based on limited experience.

*When that decision eventually turns out to be a mistake, we must learn the lesson that is to be taught through the pain of that mistake. Although, true, experience begets wisdom, it doesn't have to be **your** experience from where the wisdom is extracted. Why not learn from the mistakes of someone else who has attained that wisdom already because they already had that experience?*

Success leaves clues. Find someone who is doing what you want to do and doing it at a high level, someone who has achieved success in that thing and find out how they did it. Extract what you can use from their model, fine-tune it to fit what you're doing and skip the trial and error stage and avoid the pitfalls along the way.

You don't always have to be a guinea pig and try something to see the result. In my experience, I have found that, at least among my fellow millennials, we are often bullheaded and are quick to dismiss the experience of others and have to try it for ourselves. Sometimes this works out for us but oftentimes, it doesn't. There have been many before us who have tried and failed or tried and succeeded in most everything you can think up. The refusal to seek the counsel of wise men could result in unnecessary setbacks and difficulties for you. In the same breath, I caution you not to allow anyone to project their fears upon you and cause you not to take a chance on yourself just because they didn't succeed.

You can learn from others' experiences without taking on their perceived fears.

*Be mindful, when taking another's advice, ensure that their advice is aligned with your **clearly defined** mission and goals and does not compromise your integrity or what you know to be righteous. If, in any way, one's advice is not aligned with that which is good, if it's based in anything other than love, I'd encourage you to stay far away from it.*

CHAPTER 6 - SECOND SON

On March 6, 1993, my great aunt, AV, came to rescue us. I call it a rescue because for four children who knew nothing other than being together, the foster system was perilous for us. I don't know if we would have survived it apart from one another. My sister Ciara was being abused, I was being abused, and the separation was hurting us more than anything. And the system?! Don't get me started on the system. It was an EPIC FAILURE. It failed us in almost every way possible. It's no secret that DYFS has been hit with lawsuits and other troubles. I think our case worker, Brenda Craig, did the best she could for us, but she could only do what the system would allow.

AV was the same aunt who took me in when my mother gave me away after I was born. She was forty-five years old, struggling emotionally with her divorce and living by herself on a limited income. Yet, she instantly became the mother of four children between the ages of five and eleven years old. We were finally together again, as a family, and my sisters and I were on top of the world. AV was fond of all her nieces and nephews but she'll admit, there was just always something about "Tracey's kids," and more so, something special about me that she always loved.

We were so happy. Our lives were somewhat normal again. The only thing missing now was our mom. AV let us see her from time to time. Some people in the family would try to tell AV it wasn't a good idea because it enabled our mother to continue to live a destructive lifestyle while someone else took care of her children. For some reason, people were under the impression that if you punished Tracey by keeping her away from her children, she'd get herself clean. Laughable. She lost us to DYFS for six months. If she wanted to get clean she would have. AV always followed her heart regardless of what everyone else said. She continued to let us see our mom every now and again.

We had it so sweet at AV's. And although things appeared to be great and everyone was happy, there was just something about me that just refused to follow the rules. I refused to be obedient, refused to comply. I was in school acting a fool, as AV would say. I don't even remember all the things I was doing but the teachers were constantly calling AV at work telling her about my behavior. I just wouldn't stay in my seat, I was always talking, always playing with friends, throwing trash across the room at friends, playing trash can basketball, etc. Sometimes, AV would have to come up to the school to deal with me, personally and pop me on my butt in front of everyone. But nothing seemed to work. She had done all that she could to convince me to behave. In her mind, she had exhausted all options.

After missing countless hours from work to come to the school to deal with my disciplinary issues, AV promised me that if she had to come back one more time, she was putting me back into the foster care system. I was really hurting her. She could not understand why I just wouldn't do right. She did nothing but show me love. When my own family put us in the system because my parents refused to stop abusing drugs and alcohol, AV rescued me. How could I just keep treating her like crap? She deserved better. I wish I knew why I was the way I was. It's still a conundrum to me. If there was one thing you could take to the bank, it was AV's promises. AV always made good on her promises. In a recent discussion with her, she said that even if she knew she made a bad decision, she would stick to it just because she made the promise to do a specific thing under specific circumstances. She valued her word more than what others thought was 'right.' She never made a promise to me that she didn't keep. One day at school, during lunch, I took my milk container and shot it in the basketball goal on my way to the trashcan. I wasn't supposed to be up out of my seat. Miss Morgan, yelled TRAAAVIS!

I'll never forget Miss Morgan. She was taller than most women. She always wore these long, fake fingernails and she was always chewing her gum loudly. AV had made it known throughout the school, and all the teachers knew, if anyone calls her up to the school again for something that I did, I was going back into the system. Mrs. Fisher tried to protect me. She always did love me. Even Mrs. Ragsdale tried to work with me and I was always a thorn in her side. "Don't make me call your Aunt," most teachers would say to me, and I'd usually straighten up. But not Miss Morgan. The first opportunity she got, Miss Morgan called AV. I felt like she never liked me. She would always find a reason to yell at me. Then again, I was always giving her a reason to yell at me.

AV came back up to the school again. She spoke to Miss Morgan and took me home. She was angry on the way home but when we got home, she broke down and cried as she told me that she had to let me go. I could see the pain that I had caused her, and the confusion on her face, trying to figure out what was wrong with me. I was not a well-behaved child.

Besides my mother, I don't think anyone loved me as much as AV. So, when she made the decision to put me back in the system, she felt she had no other recourse. I was hurting our family. For AV, missing time from work was missing money. She lived on a one-person income and took on four children. She couldn't afford to miss time from work. Sometimes you must cut off the finger to save the hand. And it wasn't like she gave up on me quickly. She endured this for a couple of years. I think I was about ten years old by now. My behavior, by that point, was unacceptable and inexcusable. I should have known better. I did know better. I just chose to do what I wanted, when I wanted. Including my mother, people were always making excuses for me—using my age, my trauma and my broken home as an excuse for my behavior. Still, at that age, you know right from wrong. You make choices at that age and you can choose to make the right ones. I saw kids who didn't want to get into trouble in class choose to sit in their seats, choose to listen to the teacher, choose to be model students, so I could have also. They weren't any more brilliant than I. I just didn't make the correct choices like they did. I preferred to be the class clown.

'I had beaten the system before. There was no way I would ever again get my ass whooped by a foster parent like I did when I was younger. I was a kid then, I wish somebody would try to beat me now. I'm ten! There was no way I was going to get starved, physically or emotionally abused. I conquered it before, it was only six months. I'll be back with AV again shortly. I just have to be good and wait this one out. If I'm good, things will be easy and I'll be back home with my sisters in no time! Piece of cake. I've got this.' Or so I thought. In Sicklerville, NJ, as I lay my head down on the pillow for the first night as the new son of Maggie and Hodges Hall, it hit me like a ton of bricks. I'm back in the system.

I cried uncontrollably that night. I missed Sarina, Ciara and Tiona. I missed my Mom. I was angry with AV but I missed her too. How could she do this to me?! Of course, I never looked at myself as the problem that I was. I just blamed everyone else. My youthful ignorance prevented me from seeing the problem I was. I was every parent's worst nightmare—breaking stuff, getting into fights in school, talking back, setting fires, writing on walls and lying. You could catch me red-handed and I would stick to that lie so good, you'd end up believing it. I was so good at lying I would believe myself! "I need to chill, man," I said aloud to myself. "I need to get my act together or AV won't ever take me back."

This time in the system would be different from any other. I had it good in my third foster home. The Hall family truly loved me and I loved them. Though I called her Aunt Maggie, because I could not bring myself to call anyone else mom except for my mother, Maggie Hall was a great mother to me. She truly loved me. I had the things that I wanted and needed. She wanted to adopt me, but I told her I didn't want that because I thought she'd move to another state and I'd never see my family again.

Hodges was a good father, stern but fair. He didn't speak much, but he was wise. I didn't realize it at the time but, when I got older, I remembered and understood the things he tried to teach me. Kendrick, Maggie's son, was my "big brother Kendrick." Until now, I never had a big brother, so this was great. Someone I could talk to, someone I could play fight with, someone to whoop my butt in Techmo Bowl. Kendrick was cool. He was a great brother and friend to me.

I was smaller than most kids my age everywhere I went. Sometimes, kids would pick on me on the bus or in school but my life struggles had made me fearless. After everything that I had been through, getting beat up couldn't possibly be that bad. I was fearless. It was a welcomed challenge to take on the big kid who was trying to bully me.

So, when a neighborhood kid, who happened to be white, told me he was going to knock me out with his "n— beaters," all my memories of getting attacked by racist kids from Oakview Elementary came rushing back to me. Not only did this kid threaten me, but he made it racial. The town of Lawnside had a 98% African American population, so I hadn't experienced racism in a while. I became blind with rage and went after him like a wild bull, right in his front yard. None of his friends could get me off him.

Uncle Hodges came down the street and stopped the fight. I tried to explain to him what happened, but he didn't want to hear it. He was upset with me for fighting. He just wouldn't listen and wouldn't let me explain. My pride was hurt, I'm in a fight, I've got the upper hand and then my "Dad" comes and pulls me off the kid and embarrasses me! But I was embarrassing him with my behavior. He was so embarrassed by how I was acting, he told the other kids and parents there that he was going to call my caseworker and he mentioned I was a foster child. I felt betrayed and unloved. We had an agreement in my foster family, that no one would tell anyone I was a foster child. That was embarrassing to me. I already had kids trying to pick with me for the color of my skin, my height and my behavior. I didn't need them having more fuel for the fire. I yelled out, "I want to leave!"

Now, Uncle Hodges had a lot of pride too, for sure. I wasn't backing down and he wasn't backing down. He also didn't want to hold me against my will, and I said I wanted to go. By the end of the night, I regretted everything I had done and said. My bags were packed and my caseworker was sitting on the living room couch. Aunt Maggie was at work when this all happened and I didn't even get a chance to see her face and say goodbye. If she had just gotten one more chance to look at me, she would have made sure I didn't go anywhere. To this day, she still grieves that evening.

The first saddest day of my life was when my family placed us in the foster care system. My second saddest day was when AV put me back into the system. This day replaced the second saddest day. I had it so good there, everything I wanted and needed, but I was off to the next home. What would happen next would change my life, forever.

The Decision is Theirs

Of course, while going through all of this, I couldn't help but to think about my mother. Doesn't she love me? Doesn't she know I'm getting bounced around? Why won't she get clean? I once asked my mother, while sitting on the steps in Nana's house,

"Mom, do you love me?"

"Of course, I do, baby, I will always love you!"

"Would you stop doing drugs for me?"

Her reply was honest, yet devastating. She simply said, "Baby, I'm not ready." As a twelve-year-old boy, who's always missed his mother, that comment destroyed me, emotionally. I felt like my mother didn't love me as much as she loved getting high. That affected me my entire life up until I was thirty years old and I actually forgave her. The point is, a person will only stop doing drugs when they're ready; when they've made the choice to stop. There is nothing that you can do or say to make them stop. Even if you say something that makes them consider stopping, it is still ultimately their decision.

I know you're struggling with not having your parents around because of their addiction to drugs. I know you blame yourself sometimes for their addiction. I know you hate them for not being there for you and forcing you to grow up sooner than you should have. You blame them for your perceived proclivity to become a drug addict yourself. You question why they don't love you enough to quit. You question if there is anything you can do to get them off drugs. You think maybe if you just showed them or show them more love, things would be different. For your own sake, I implore you, stop blaming yourself for things which you have no control. Ultimately, the decision is theirs

I have taken my mother to programs and left her there after I signed her in. Often, within 72 hours, she was calling me, cursing me out because I dropped her off at a program and she wasn't ready to quit using drugs. Sometimes, she was calling me from home because she had somehow escaped from the rehab. People will not quit until they have made the decision for themselves to quit. And if you force them into a program and they complete it, they still will not stay clean until they make the decision to do so.

They need to understand that they have the power, the power given to them by God, to decide to overcome their addiction. By giving power to physiological/physical illness, they are not acknowledging the God power in them. I, personally, will not accept or believe any physiological, physical or psychological influence has that much power and dominion over me and my life.

I know you want your loved one clean, but the truth is, they may not ever get clean. But you still owe it to yourself to lead a happy and fulfilled life. And if you wait for them or blame them for your inability to cope or blame them for your emotional issues, you'll forever be pointing the finger. If your life fails, YOU FAILED YOU! No one else. SAVE YOURSELF! If your life ends up being turned upside down, that drug addict parent of yours sure won't be able to save you. When I needed someone's help, my parents, in their addiction, were nowhere to be found. I had to save myself. And when they were going through their addiction, I couldn't help them. Today, at thirty-three years old, I still have to save myself. Today, I don't just owe it to me, I owe it to my wife and to my children who don't deserve a husband and a father in their lives who can't cope because he's stuck in 1992 and blames his life on the decisions his parents made almost 25 years ago!

I had to forgive my parents before I could truly tap into my power to free myself from the bonds of blame and resentment. And I had to forgive them without expecting them to apologize to me or somehow make up for any lost time. I had to just let go of any resentment I had toward them for the things I felt they did to me.

I won't preach to you about forgiveness, but I will say this: once I forgave my parents for what I felt was something they had done to me, I actually realized that they were not the reason for my trauma or the reason my emotional state was in shambles, disorder and dis-ease. After I forgave them, I could finally see that I was solely responsible for my life's circumstances because I was solely responsible for my decisions. Once I took hold of my life, stopped blaming everyone else and took responsibility for my circumstances, I realized that I had the power to change them. It was the great Irish playwright George Bernard Shaw who said "The people who get on in this world are the people who get up and look for the circumstances they want and if they can't find them, they create them."

CHAPTER 7 - UNTITLED

Everything happens by design. Nothing is accidental, nothing is happenstance, everything is purposeful and intentional and life happens for you, not to you. Had the things that occurred in my life not occured, I wouldn't be who I am today. So, for all that has transpired in my life, I AM grateful.

1995. Chesilhurst, NJ. I was eleven years old. Things were terrible. The Halls used to let me call my family from time to time. My new foster parents wouldn't even let me go near the phone. I hated them. They didn't try to make me feel like I was part of a family. They barely even talked to me. They only acknowledged me when I asked for food or when my foster mother needed help getting up from the couch. She'd let herself go so badly that she was too heavy to get up on her own. Other than that, I barely existed. All the foster parents cared about was getting that check from the state for me being there but that money wasn't being spent on me. I was still wearing the same sneakers from my last foster home and they didn't buy me any new clothes. Almost every dinner was microwaved and I hardly ever got to have cereal for breakfast because half the time, the milk was sour. I hated it there but I had a roof over my head. Things could have been worse.

The foster parents had been talking about getting another foster child, a boy. I was hoping he'd be my age because I'd never had a brother my age to play with. Or maybe a big brother like Kendrick. The much-anticipated day finally arrived and I stood on the couch and looked out the window all morning. Around noon my foster mother told me to put some hot dogs on the stove for myself for lunch. This was strange because she normally didn't care if I fed myself or not. Just as I was about to sit down to eat, there was a knock on the door. I helped my foster mother off the couch so she could open the creaky, rusty-hinged door. The first thing I saw was a young man staring down at the ground. As the door opened wider he looked up slowly, first with eyes, then his head, as a sly, faux smile formed on his face. My feeling of excitement disappeared almost immediately. I didn't like this kid. He was way older than me and he looked mean.

"Hi, how are you? This is Jason," said the caseworker as she beamed. She had to be the happiest person in the room that day; probably because she was getting rid of him. Jason walked through the door and stood in the living room, facing the couch (where my foster mother was already sitting back down). He looked eerily familiar but I couldn't place him so, I didn't give it a second thought. Jason and I didn't have much interaction the first few days he was there. He stayed to himself, mostly. Then, one day, I overheard him having a conversation with the foster parents. As I walked into the living room, Jason was telling them he knew me from Lawnside and he used to hang with my cousins. He told them I used to lie and steal all the time.

I quickly interjected to defend myself, but my foster mother shut me down. I didn't know this kid or why was he lying on me. They were all laughing as Jason told jokes at my expense. I was enraged; my defense mechanism for hurt was anger, but I was fighting back tears because I didn't want them to see they'd gotten to me. Then I remembered. I'd seen Jason before, with the older kids. He was the outcast. No one really liked this guy because he was a habitual liar. He was a boxer, he was Puff Daddy's cousin, he was cousins to one of my cousins; he was a fraud. That's what he was. I was always cool with the older guys because my cousin Tanya, who used to babysit me, would sometimes take me with her when she hung with them. Other than that, I didn't hang out much with the older guys and I didn't personally know Jason outside of hearing other people say he was a liar and "cornball." But why was he lying on me? I would later find out that Jason was painting a picture of me that would destroy my credibility because Jason had plans.

Everything was fine before Jason came. Well, "fine," of course, is relative. By "fine" I mean I didn't have many issues. But, after Jason showed up, Rob's Rolex watch went missing. Not long after that, a pocketknife went missing. And finally, $100 disappeared from Rob's wallet. Rob was the foster mother's brother. He was cool. He used to watch me from time to time and he would take me out to throw the football around in the yard. He was hilarious and could always make me laugh.

At eleven years old, I didn't understand the value of a Rolex. I couldn't spend $100 because I couldn't go anywhere, the property was on a large piece of land surrounded by wooded area. The closest store to us was a liquor store, which I couldn't go into. There was no sidewalk and I wasn't allowed off the property. Now to be totally transparent, before I moved with AV, I stole things. My mother would send us off while in stores and I'd go steal candy and toys while she'd steal bigger things like packs of meat and loaves of bread. Sometimes, I just stole for the thrill of it. But when I moved with AV, she let me know she would break my little fingers if I stole and embarrassed her in a store. So, I stopped stealing. I liked my fingers. AV provided everything we needed and wanted, anyway, so there was no need to steal.

As things were going missing, I was a prime suspect. Jason had told the foster parents that I was a liar and a thief. I remember literally begging the foster parents to believe that I didn't steal anything and, while I was crying and pleading, Jason was standing behind me yelling "Yes you did." You stole it!" "Yes you did!" I pushed him away angrily, "See!" he said, "Told you he stole it! That's why he's so mad!" That night, we never got to the bottom of who the thief was, but I'm sure they thought it was me.

We shared a room with bunkbeds. One night Jason came down from the top bunk, as he often did in the middle of the night. He'd usually leave the room for a little bit then come back. I never even considered why he was getting up but, if I had to guess at that time, I would guess he was going to the bathroom. Hindsight being 20/20, it would be a safe bet to guess he was creeping around the house stealing things. But one particular night he got down off his bunk would change the course of my life, forever.

Getting down from the top bunk, Jason stepped on the bottom bunk, as he always did. As always, it woke me but, this time, oddly, I didn't hear the door open. I noticed he wasn't leaving the room, so I turned over. He was standing in front of me, on the side of the bed, completely naked. He grabbed my head with both of his hands and attempted to pull my face into his groin area. "Suck it, you know you want to." I didn't have my sticks in my pants and my rocks in my pockets but I was ready for the fight of my life. I was not going to be a victim. I punched and kicked and yelled "Stop, get off me!" Surprisingly, he just backed off. As he climbed back onto the top bunk, in a muffled yell, I heard "Shut up, I'm just f— with you," and he laughed. Then he leaned over the top bunk with a pocket knife in his right hand and said "You know they put me here cuz I'm crazy, right?" I wasn't sure what that meant, but I had a pretty good guess. After all, he was on daily medication and he just showed me how crazy he could be. I was afraid to move. I was afraid to yell. But I was more afraid that he was going to come back down off that bed and what would happen if he did.

I ran out the bedroom and across the hall to the foster parents' room and told them what just happened. I turned the light on and woke them up. As they yelled at me for waking them up, I immediately started talking. I was having trouble getting the words out because I was extremely emotional and crying uncontrollably. I'll never forget the look the foster father's face. After he rolled over, he didn't move, he just laid there and stared at me, like either he was asleep with his eyes open or he was dead and frozen in that position.

After I finished the story, he shook his head and closed his eyes. The foster mother took a deep breath, shook her head, sucked her teeth, sat up and dropped her legs off the side of the bed. "Hand me my slippers boy," she said as she stuck her hands in her hair and violently scratched her scalp; "waking me up with this bulls—!" She slipped her swollen feet into her house shoes and slid one foot at a time slowly across the floor until she walked into the bedroom that Jason and I shared. "What happened in here boy?" she said to

48

Jason. "Travis jumped on my bed and started punching me in my sleep so I slapped him in the head." he told her. Satisfied with his response, I assume, she then asked, "And why the hell are you naked?" He told her, "When it's hot I always sleep naked." His tone was defensive and aggressive, daring her to challenge his response.

In an awkward moment of silence, I watched her, waiting for her to do something drastic. I was expecting her to beat him or call his caseworker and have him removed or call the police or something! As I stared at her in anticipation, she looked frustrated and defeated. Her shoulders dropped as she shook her head. She took one final deep breath, threw her hands up and said just three words... "Stop wrasslin 'round." She turned toward the door and she slowly slid one foot at a time across the floor until she got to her room and slammed the door. The term "adding insult to injury" doesn't do justice to what I had just experienced. She didn't address anything I told her about the knife Jason had, or the groin thing he did. I thought to myself, Stop wrasslin 'round?! What the f—?! This is either the damn Twilight Zone or a terrible dream!" Jason created a situation where I had zero credibility by telling these people that I was a liar and a thief. Either that or they really just didn't care. I want to believe it was the former, but realistically, it was likely a combination of the two and probably more of the latter. Either way, this just empowered Jason. He felt like he could do whatever he wanted to, now. And quite frankly, I thought he could too. I didn't sleep the rest of that night nor many other nights after. I honestly don't think I even want to remember how many times it happened. I'm barely holding it together as I'm writing this and recalling the terror of those nights.

We had to play outside every day for at least two hours. It was mandatory as long as it wasn't raining. When the foster parents sent us outside I was always the first one out. I had to get a head start on Jason and find a good hiding spot in one of the trees or in the ditch I was digging that I covered with leaves and sticks. I'd hide by the pond with the cattails surrounding it or I'd run around the back of the house and watch him run out searching for me. Sometimes, I'd just run deep into the woods farther than I thought Jason would believe I'd go. I couldn't get complacent and lazy because once Jason got outside, he'd be hunting for me.

Every time I saw him, while I was hiding, he had the pocket knife, an axe or a machete in his hand. The foster father used the axe for chopping wood in the front yard and Jason stole the knife from the foster mother's brother—(he most likely stole the money and the Rolex too)—but the machete?! I don't know where the hell he got that from. From high in the trees I'd see him walking through the tall grass in the woods with a machete. I mean, I know his name was "Jason," but c'mon. This was literally like a scene out of a horror movie.

He would hunt for me from the time we went outside until the two hours was up and it was time to go back inside. When the two hours of mandatory outside time was over, I would make a beeline straight for the house running as fast as I could. There were only two paths to the house from the woods. Once I got to the house I was safe, but the trick was choosing the right path. Every once in a while, Jason would see me or hear me running through the tall grass and he'd start chasing behind me. I wasn't one of those idiots in the scary movies who fall and trip over his/her own feet while running from the machete-wielding psychopath. I was fast as hell and Jason was actually a bit on the heavier and slow side. Usually, I'd outrun him.

As scary as this game of cat and mouse was, as scary as the knife, axe and the machete were, the scariest thing about this whole situation was that I wasn't running for my "life." I actually kind of wish I was. Every now and again, Jason would pick the path I was running down and he'd hide in the tall grass or behind some trees and pop out and tackle me on my route to the house. When Jason outwitted me and caught me in the woods, when no one was watching... well...

Imagine yourself, at eleven years old. What was your life like? What were you doing? Where were you? Did your parents put you to bed and kiss you on the forehead as they said good night and whispered "I love you?" Did you wake up in the morning to the smell of mom's breakfast as you roll over and see the sun shining through the blinds and the birds chirping outside? Now, imagine yourself an eleven-year-old boy, who's always felt abandoned by his family, lonely and unloved. Your own family has abandoned you, given up on you and twice placed you into a failed system that's supposed to give children like you a chance at a normal life. But your life isn't normal. You've never had real friends. You've never been in one place long enough to develop your first crush. You don't even remember what it's like to get a hug from someone who loves you. The life you wish you had with your mother and sisters, happy and together again, you can only see in your dreams.

And just when you're most vulnerable, lonely, and broken you begin to dream of that happy life with your family. Then suddenly you're jolted out of your sleep by a sixteen-year-old young man who's lying on your back, kissing your neck. With one hand, he's covering your mouth, whispering in your ear, "You scream, I'll f— kill you," and with the other hand he inserts his saliva-lubricated anatomy inside of you with no regard for the muffled screams from your gut wrenching anguish and pain. You can feel his breath, it's hot. You can smell his body odor, like freshly chopped onions, he's sweating profusely. You can taste your own blood; your lip is busted. You're weak, you can't get him off you and every time you move it hurts more. You beg him to stop. He ignores you.

Accepting defeat, you know all you can do is hope it ends soon. As he reaches his climax, he thrusts his hips forward with all his might. It causes you agonizing pain like you've never felt before. You scream as loud as you can but his hand is covering your mouth and no one hears you. It wouldn't have mattered anyway; the pain was so excruciating your breath was snatched away and your scream was just a muffled gasp. All you see is white... then black and the next thing you know... you wake up.

The sun is shining through the blinds, the birds are chirping outside and you're hoping you just had a nightmare. You convince yourself it was a dream but you taste the dry blood on your bottom lip. Your underwear are around your ankles and you're in pain. I've never felt so weak in all my life. As I heard Jason moving around on the top bunk, stricken with fear, I curled up in the corner of my bed, my knees to my chest, and I bawled uncontrollably. I couldn't move, I couldn't speak and I couldn't make a sound. I was just a kid who missed his mom, who grew up without his dad and was thrown into the system by his own family. I didn't ask for this life. Why did I deserve this?

Now, imagine being chased through the woods by a knife wielding, sixteen-year-old, psychopath rapist when no one can hear your cries for help and your foster parents don't believe you when you try to tell them what's going on. Imagine running through the cattails, too afraid to look back after you see him see you, then you feel his hand on your shoulder.

You instantly lose all hope as, on your other shoulder, you feel the point of that pocket knife pressing against your skin as Jason dares you keep up the fight. Can you imagine being able to see your home just over the cattails, knowing you were so close to making it to safety, and all you could do, while having what's left of your innocence stripped away from you, is cry for you mom? I don't know what was worse, having this happen to me and having to cry for my mother because there was nothing else I could do, or knowing she nor anyone else was ever coming to rescue me. I don't know if there's a greater feeling of despair.

Eventually, I got tired of being a victim. I got tired of crying for my mother while Jason held a knife to me while having his way. My mom wasn't coming for me. I got tired of wishing my dad taught me how to fight so I could defend myself. My daddy wasn't coming to save me. I made up in my mind that I would not be a victim ever again. I realized that I was the one person that was going to change my circumstances. So, either I was going to roll over and die or I was going to kill Jason… figuratively or literally.

One day, my two hours of being outside was almost up, I'm lying on the ground, hiding in the cattails by the pond, when Jason spotted me. As he slowly walked up on me, seeing I had no intention on running, he put down the axe, and quickly pulled down his sweatpants. What Jason didn't know was that when I saw him walking my way, there was a reason I didn't run. I had made the decision that I was not going to be his victim any longer. I was determined not to lose. This time, I had my sticks, I had my rocks and I gave him the fight of my life! I wasn't going to run! I roundhouse kicked his ass right into the pond... and then I ran.

I made it to the house screaming for the foster parents, Jason was close behind me with the axe held high, threatening to kill me. Rob saw this from the window and heard me screaming. He ran outside and grabbed the axe from Jason. I told him, and my foster parents, that Jason was trying to kill me and I wanted to leave. Too embarrassed and ashamed to tell them what he had been doing to me all these weeks, and since they ignored me previously when I tried to tell them, I just begged them to let me leave. Even though I pleaded with them, tears streaming down my face, sobbing uncontrollably with my hands clutched together, at my chin, fingers interlocked and begging with all that was within me, they wouldn't let me go. I begged to call my caseworker, but they refused to let me make the call.

Foster children are guaranteed money from the state. That was all they cared about. It was clear that they weren't letting me go anywhere but I was determined not to lose. I wasn't going to give Jason anymore opportunities to victimize me. I was getting out of here one way or another.

I took matches with me to the woods. As I struck the match against the striking surface, I stared at the flame, contemplating whether I was doing the right thing. I rationalized my actions by acknowledging the fact we lived right next door to the firehouse. As the blaze started to grow, I felt a smile come across my face, I dropped the book of matches in the flames just to make sure the fire didn't go out and then I ran to the house. Not because I was afraid of the fire, but because I couldn't wait to tell them what I had done. I knew they had to let me out of there now! I knew the police would come and I could tell them what was happening to me and they'd have to take me away. Needless to say, I was out of there—in a group home for behaviorally challenged children, but I was out of there.

The first go around in the foster care system was tough, I was abused physically, and mentally, starved and beaten. I didn't come out unscathed, but I came out victorious. Sure, I ate a little dog food. The beatings and the hunger pains didn't hurt me as much as the void in my heart from not having my mother. When AV got me out, I was with family again, and to me, that was a win! My family turned their backs on me and shoved me into the system. Coming out with only limited trauma was a win in my mind.

But round 2… round 2 in the system was totally different. The rules had changed. It was no holds barred. This was a different arena; a different game altogether. The opposing team was stacked, they called in the ringers, the refs missed every foul and I was given no timeouts to use. The system beat me this time. Not only did it beat me, it broke me. It literally raped and robbed me of what was left of my innocence and destroyed me emotionally.

Travis 1, Foster Care 1.

Tie Game

When I Stopped Being a "Victim"

The "victim's mentality" is one that is developed, acquired after an individual has been "victimized"—affected in some way, usually negatively by the actions of another. In my case, the victim's mentality purported itself in such a way that it served as an excuse for me to engage in inexcusable behavior, and to feel blameless in my actions, especially ones that were not based in morality. "Victims" who are plagued by this way of thinking believe that it also excuses them from procuring for themselves the life they deserve. Instead, we ultimately settle for a less desirable lifestyle and accept failure in some instances, deferring the blame for our lack of success, happiness and fulfilment and placing it on others or our "victimization."

*Until I was twenty-seven years old, I didn't realize that because of my traumatic experience at age eleven, I had developed a victim's mentality. It affected my decisions, it affected my attitude and it gave me permission to fail. It gave me an excuse to be held back and to hate. It was justification for me being unhappy and unfulfilled. I blamed my mother and father for **my** life's circumstances as if **their** addictions were the cause for **my** crappy life. The thought of it is ridiculous! I ignored the fact that my actions and choices had everything to do with creating my undesired circumstances. A lot of us actually feel this way about people in our lives. Battered women, rape victims, victims of abuse, etc., are sometimes crippled by their victimizations and often we blame the situations, events, people and especially our abusers for our inaction or circumstances in life. Yes, these things definitely contributed to some of my pain and my fears; they absolutely did, but, that's because of how I interpreted the action. I interpreted my victimization as something that would make it difficult for me to cope in some areas of my life— therefore it did. Once I realized that I was the only person responsible for MY life's circumstances, things in MY life began to change for the better because I made the decision that they would. I believed that they would. And I did the* *work necessary to ensure that they did. It's surely reasonable to blame the doer of a thing for their actions. But, blaming other things and people for MY life's circumstances only empowered my inaction. Taking responsibility for my own life empowered me to act and to change the things that were non-desirable in my life.*

I blamed the police officer and his blatantly racist comment and untruths in his reporting for the reason I was arrested and couldn't get a job as a police officer, rather than blaming my own actions which, truly precipitated the arrest. I blamed my Nana for telling me since the age of 7 that I would end up dead or in jail just like my father for the reason I almost ended up dead multiple times and in cells like my father. I blamed the "system" for why I couldn't get the job I wanted. I blamed the teacher for my F in dance class in college. I blamed my attacker for why I couldn't have a normal relationship with my wife. Do you see the pattern? When I saw myself as a victim, I was one. The same with the man who believes he is a victor; if he believes he's an overcomer, then he is and he will be.

For as a man thinks in his heart, so is he.
—Proverbs 23:7 (KJV)

By thinking I was a victim, I was destined to do, have and feel what victims do, have and feel. When I stopped being a victim, by refusing to accept and believe that I was, I simultaneously decided that I would be an overcomer. I then intentionally and deliberately began thinking, saying and doing what overcomers think, say and do. Making this decision was the first step to becoming a victor. No longer thinking I was a victim, I became empowered. And surely enough, I began to win. I began to succeed.

With the decision to go from victim to victor, I took control of my life. I could finally have a normal physical relationship with my wife. I could finally get the job I wanted. I could finally become successful in whatever endeavor I chose to pursue. I finally started to win. If you don't choose to shift your paradigm—change your system of beliefs, your outlook on life and the way of perceiving, understanding and doing things, you have essentially made the choice to suffer, to fail, to lose. Don't you want to have the life you always wanted? Don't you want to be happy and fulfilled? YOU CAN. If you CHOOSE to. You can have the life you desire, the happiness you yearn for and the fulfilment you deserve. But you MUST choose to. Being responsible, I must acknowledge the fact that some things may not come as easy to some as for others. Your trauma may appear to be more difficult to overcome than mine or someone else's. Fulfillment is not a switch you click and you just automatically have it. No, you must continue to work for what you want. You may not see sweeping change occur immediately, but if you stay the course and become determined not to lose, and you choose only to have the results that you desire, no matter what, you'll eventually have them.

The book "The Slight Edge," by Jeff Olsen teaches us that only 5% of people will reach their desired level of success in their lifetime. Those individuals, the 5%, when faced with the decision to make either simple disciplined decisions or simple errors in judgement, choose to make the disciplined decisions. Those decisions, compounded over time equate to them achieving success. The other 95%, when faced with the same type of decision, choose to make simple errors in judgement that, compounded over time, cause their life to end up in failure. Of that 95%, what percentage do you think claim to be "victims?" By "victim," I mean, one who: instead of finding a solution to their problems or circumstances, they complain about what others are doing or have done to them that precludes them from making progress in any specific area of their life. They consistently talk about what others do or have done to keep them from overcoming and succeeding. Instead of looking in the mirror, they blame someone else for their problems.

Instead of eating healthy, the victim eats unhealthy and blames their slow metabolism for the fact that they're "big boned." They say "obesity runs in the family" and that's the reason for them being overweight. This is the pattern we get into when we have the victim's mentality.

Let's look at our circle of influence, look at the people around us, our friends... think about the last time we complained to them. Didn't they complain with us? They validated our complaint with either a complaint of their own or a "I hear you girl," "Tell me about, man," or "Yea it is too hard!" It's easier to give up and give in than it is to face our fears, face our victimization and develop a MUST win attitude. By the way, "victims" love to be consoled by other "victims." But just as misery loves company, positivity attracts positivity. We must get away from those other "victims," the complainers and the nay-sayers and get around some positive people. Otherwise, we'll stay stuck in the "victim's mindset."

When you MUST win and you MUST overcome, no victimization, no excuse, no perceived lack of finances, energy or time will keep you from your goal. If someone told you "you MUST get a job or you'll die," you'd get that job. You'd be at McDonald's faster than you can say "two all-beef patties, special sauce, lettuce cheese, pickles, onions on a sesame seed bun!" Well, I'm telling you, if you don't develop a MUST WIN mindset, you will die... unhappy, unfulfilled and full of regret.

We must embrace what we consider our "victimization." What happened to us actually happened for us. It happened so we could become the person we are meant to become. You are an overcomer. You are stronger and more powerful than you realize, and part of it is because of what happened for you. You were built to be able to handle anything that comes your way. You survived what you survived. You're a survivor! Embrace it. I overcame my victimization emotionally by believing God had purpose for me enduring what I did. And by embracing it and using it to help others overcome their victimizations, I was able to take dominion over mine.

Take a moment to complete this exercise:

On a piece of paper, write down some of your life's circumstances that are undesirable at this present moment. Number the list. Maybe your relationship is not so great, your finances aren't in order, you don't have the car you desire or you haven't gotten the raise or promotion you want at work, your mother-in law dislikes you; maybe your business is struggling or your ministry is not taking off like you want, etc.

On another sheet of paper, write down the cause(s) for each of your undesirable circumstances. If any of your causes are extrinsic factors (outside forces), cross them out and find a solely intrinsic cause (operating from within)—something that you did or did not do that bears the responsibility for that undesirable circumstance.

Finally, on one more separate sheet of paper, write down the immediate actions YOU can take to change the trajectory of your life. What can you do, right now, to change those circumstances? If YOU don't change, your life will not change. You cannot change someone else. You will not change someone else. But if YOU change YOU and your actions, You WILL change YOUR circumstances.

CHAPTER 8 - SPARE THE ROD

One of the last things my grandmother, Barbara Marie Peterkin-Davis said to my father was the single greatest thing she had ever done for me. From her deathbed, she uttered to her son, "Make sure you take care of them kids." Words my father would never forget, they endured through his addictions and lifestyle and ensured that one day, he'd make sure he took care of his kids.

After getting placed in the group home, I had no faith in my life changing for the better. I felt like I was just like another institutionalized kid. A lonely orphan who no one cared about. But one day I got word that my father was going to be coming to get me soon. At that time, even though I was angry with my father, I was just happy that someone in my family was coming to rescue me and take me away from this awful place so I could feel like a normal person again.

It was 1995 when my father finally got me out of the group home. He convinced AV to get temporary custody of me while he got the paperwork and custody issues sorted out. Eventually I was living with him in his apartment in Colwyn, PA, right outside of Darby. When I first started living there and my father had to go to work, Grandpop Al would babysit me. The only thing that changed about Grandpop Al since I last remembered seeing him back in 1987 was that he wasn't working, anymore.

He would still get up early, get his orange juice and vodka, put on some Johnny Cash or Hank Williams records, turn on the television and sit down on the couch. When I arrived at his house, that's where I would find him, waiting for me. My grandfather adored me. He was very kind to me. As my mother says, "He loved himself some Travis!" He loved when I came over to spend time with him. And boy, did he love to talk! We had some great conversations. He talked to me about my mom often, surprisingly. He'd sound remorseful about what I had to experience as a youth and say "Your father never should have beat your mother like that.

I always told his a—, girls ain't nothin' but trouble." Maybe Grand pop Al didn't know I had very vivid memories of him encouraging my father to strike my mother. My dad said he didn't want to beat my mother when his father would tell him to do it. My father blamed his father and his father blamed him. It didn't matter really, he liked talking, I liked listening and I liked thinking about my mother, who I didn't see often. He'd show me pictures of her smiling, looking happy. It made me happy.

During my time living with my father, he ensured I understood the importance of education. C's were unacceptable in our home. If you got a C, you obviously didn't apply yourself. I was always smart in school, so getting the grades was easy, it was my behavior that I struggled with.

My father was a marine and he was very regimented with everything he did. He had to have absolute control over everything. It was the only way he could function. I used to think it was crazy. If the bed wasn't made with military creases, you would have thought it was the end of the world when he came home. If you didn't iron pleats into your jeans exactly like "this" (the way he showed you), you were better off dead. He had this same attitude with everything. He said to get clean, he had to rule his own life with an iron fist. Unfortunately, that was the only way he knew how to preside over the lives of others whom he was responsible.

During the week, my father went to work, I went to school and on Sunday, we went to church. Christ Haven Pentecostal Church at 6th and Walnut streets, in Darby. This was where I was first introduced to the teachings of Jesus Christ, where my spiritual relationship with God was acknowledged and where my foundation in holiness was first built.

When I was living with my first foster parent Miss Brice, we were regularly attending the Kingdom Hall of Jehovah's Witnesses but I was too young to really grasp what was going on. At Christ Haven, I was old enough to understand what I was hearing and to research what I was learning. This was where I accepted Jesus Christ as my Lord and Savior, where I was baptized and where I had the full church experience. I had some of the best times of my life there. I made some of the most amazing friends. I learned that there are people in this world who are truly invested in helping others without looking for anything in return. That there are people in this world that truly want to bless you and who, like God, love you for who you are and look beyond your faults and see your needs. I felt good here. I felt loved and I felt safe. Most importantly, I felt God.

Dad had finally gotten himself together and settled enough where he felt he could take on the responsibility of taking care of another one of his children. Tiona was with Nana and that was best for Tiona. She had a medical condition that required experimental surgery at the Children's Hospital of Philadelphia (which she'll tell you about in her book). It was best for Tiona to be in Philly, but Sarina was with AV. Since Ciara's biological mother had gotten out of prison, and been clean for years, she got custody of Ciara. Sarina was the only one left with AV. It was time for Sarina to come and live with us.

Once Sarina came to live with us, my life got so much better! Sarina and I are still, to this day, extremely close. We never fight or argue. If we disagree about something, we do so respectfully, come up with the perfect agreement for both sides and move on. My sisters and I have great relationships. Most everyone that sees us interact either loves how close we all are and they give us a compliment, or they're envious of how close we all are and give us a compliment. Either way, you cannot deny that we have a rare bond that is one to admire for certain. We have been through so much together, it has bonded us in ways that are simply inexplicable on paper. One thing we have always lived by in our relationships is that love conquers all. No matter what, we always let love prevail.

While living in Colwyn Apartments, my dad met a woman who lived in the same apartments and who had newborn twin babies, AJ and Drea, and a daughter, Ky, who was my age. In fact, we went to school together and she and I were friendly with each other. I had never seen my father happy like he was when he was with Ms. Sharon. Remember, I still couldn't call anyone mom who wasn't Bambi, even though a few people had done a hell of a job filling in. We all got a house together in Darby and suddenly, Sarina and I had a new brother and sisters and we were one big happy family and almost lived happily ever, but we didn't.

I was a habitual rule breaker. It seemed like things my dad told me to do, I did the opposite and everything he told me not to do, I did. I was lacking so terribly in the self-discipline department. My father was a tyrant and he did not play around. He told me on multiple occasions, "I will f— you up in here, boy!" I knew he didn't play but something in me didn't care who it was or what the threat was, I was a rule breaker. Everyone told me I was bad so I was. I was supposed to break the rules; I was supposed to end up dead or in jail. No one ever told me I could be a doctor or a lawyer or the president of the United States. All I knew was I was a problem child, and that's all I was.

Not to mention, I had barely any respect for my father because of what I saw him do to my mother in my younger years. I used to resent him terribly for that. What frustrated me was that he treated Ms. Sharon better than my mom. He treated my new brother and my sisters better than me and I was his first son. I felt like he loved Ky and the twins more than me. He was there for them like he was never there for me. I loved Ky and the twins so much but I was so jealous of them. They had the father that I never had at the time most crucial time for him to be in their lives. There was never any sibling rivalry. I've always loved all my brothers and sisters. But in my jealousy, I built a wall between my father and me. The wall was reinforced by my refusal to respect the rules and my disregard for him as the man of the house. Then I got mad when it seemed like he loved everyone else more than he loved me and treated them better. I mean, hindsight being as 20/20 as it is, I can kind of understand it; I was the only one giving him daily head and heart aches.

"You — ain't — just — gonna — flaunt — my — damn — rules!" he said, to the beat of the belt cracking against my butt. With his belt in hand, Dad would tell me "You get a t-shirt, one pair of underwear and one pair of shorts." He'd say this while he followed me down the stairs to my room which was in the basement. I used to start crying on the way down to set the tone. I was good at fake crying. I had done a lot of real crying in my life, so it was easy.

My father could appear to be quite heartless, especially when he was angry with you. He didn't stop beating you because you begged, he didn't stop because you promised to be good and he didn't stop because you cried. Sometimes, I'd try the combination of the three to try to get him to stop. At some point, the beatings honestly didn't hurt me. Remember when I told you I wouldn't let anyone beat compliance into me? I had built up so much anger and rage that I had no emotions toward my father at some point. I'm sure, to him, he believed he was just doing the best he knew how but to me he was oppressive as hell! And I rebelled when I was oppressed. The more I acted out, the angrier he got and the tighter he pulled the reins on me. By the time I was 15, the reigns were so tight they were choking me.

My father was loyal to Ms. Sharon, his wife. He loved her, and he loved her like I never saw him love my mom. I hated that. He would call my mother all types of "crackhead bi—" in front of Ms. Sharon, like he was trying to prove his disdain for my mom. In actuality, he was helping drive a wedge between Ms. Sharon and me. He provided the wedge, but I hammered it in. For a long time, I resented her. I started being intentionally disrespectful to her too. She didn't deserve it, really. But I would watch her turn a blind eye when she knew my dad was wrong in his interactions with me. When he would say something that wasn't true, you couldn't talk back without getting popped. So, I would look to her for help and she'd turn and look away from me. I'm sure she could recognize his rage with me and maybe she just wanted no parts of it, I don't know. Maybe she thought I deserved the tongue lashings and butt whippings. Truthfully, in my mind, there wasn't enough butt whippings in the world to make me be obedient.

I felt like my dad put Ms. Sharon before me, just like I felt he did with everyone else. "My wife, my wife..." he hardly referred to her by name. He would look me in my face and say "My wife..." I felt like he knew I hated the fact he married someone other than my mom and I felt he was throwing it in my face. And that really set me off. I started getting worse and worse and I *really* started resenting Ms. Sharon. My wife this, my wife that... One morning, while he was yelling at me about something, Ms. Sharon chimed in and I talked back to her.

All I heard was my father's feet literally running from his bedroom down the stairs. As he was coming downstairs he was yelling to me "I will kill your motherf— ass up in here before I let you disrespect my wife!" His voice cracked, he was crying as he said it, he was infuriated with that rage I've seen before. I could tell he wanted to knock my head off but he was fighting back that rage. As one single tear dripped from his eye to his top lip, he poked me in my chest with every following group of words. "Open your mouth, and disrespect my wife, again, and the police, will be dragging, your motherf— body OUT OF HERE!!!!" He walked back upstairs. I think I had mentally drained him and he was truly at his wit's end.

As he got to the top of the stairs, my anger started to boil. I felt a tear roll down my face as I thought to myself, Wait, did he just threaten to kill me, because of her?! From that very moment into the foreseeable future, it was on.

My father tried talking to me, he tired yelling at me, he tried punishments and, when all else failed, he'd try the rod of correction. My friend John lived across the street. John's mother told my dad that she found out John and I had been sneaking out in the middle of the night, walking through the neighborhood looking for mischief. Dad was infuriated. He went straight for the rod. He didn't let me go out when I wanted to go out, so I snuck out of the basement window when everyone was asleep and came back in before they woke up. By this time, my rebellion was intentional, I just didn't care anymore. "You gone sneak out of my house in the middle of the night and jeopardize the safety of my wife and kids?" he said, as he walked upstairs to get the belt.

His footsteps were heavy, like he might fall through to the basement. As he turned the corner I saw a board not the belt in his hand. In his mind, he may have been thinking he had exhausted every other option. In my mind, I've been here before, in foster care. I knew the difference between discipline and abuse. Once I saw the board, I shut down. My last thought was of my first foster mother Ms. Brice abusing me with a board and I immediately blacked out. As he hit me, I was there but I wasn't.

I didn't make a noise, I didn't move, I didn't whimper, I didn't shed a tear. I'm going to beat that attitude right out of your ass!" Dad said, as he stared into my face. When he said it, he was so close to me, the spit flew off his mouth and landed on my lip. When Dad was scolding you, you were standing at the position of attention like a soldier in the military. You better not wipe that spit off your lip, or you'd be picking up you or your lip off the ground.

"F— you!" I said, in my mind of course, but then, I said it with my body language. I stared directly into his eyes and I slowly wiped that spit off my lip! He went into a rage. He continued to hit me and hit me and eventually as I came back from wherever I went mentally when I blacked out, I started to feel the pain. That angered me even more. The more I refused to cry and stared at him, the angrier he got and the harder he hit me. That made me nervous because I've seen this rage in him before. The mixture of his blind rage and him feeling like he's lost control was the recipe for his special knuckle sandwiches. And unlike my mom, I liked my eyes. I wanted to see. So, I let a fake cry come out, that was all he wanted. He just wanted to break me. Without a word, he walked upstairs and slammed his door.

Foolishness is bound in the heart of a child; but the rod of correction shall drive it far from him. —Proverbs 22:15 (KJV)

Well, as you can likely imagine, things escalated quickly. The tension was so obvious between my father and me, it seemed like everyone was walking on eggshells. It was only a matter of time before my father truly lost it but you know what I was thinking? I wish he would. I'm not my mom. I just kept reminding myself of that. I'm not my mom! I could see it in his eyes when he poked me in the chest the other day. He wanted to punch my lights out and I couldn't wait for him to try. I had a mind to hand him a past due notice for his light bill. I was ready to cut his sh— off and put him in collections. He owed a debt for all the times he beat my mom and he pushed me off him as I tried to stop him.

I was in the gym, I was playing sports, I was getting strong and I think he knew it. I felt like he wanted to show me that he was still the man of the house. I remember him saying, once, "I don't care how many muscles you get, I'm still the f— man up in here!" I knew he had lost control mentally and emotionally with me and now, he was being threatened to lose control physically. I just needed an invitation. I owed him for all the times my mother didn't fight back and he blacked both her eyes. I owed him for all the times he wasn't there and my mother had to teach me how to hold my hands in a fight. I owed him for all the times when I had to learn how to fight in the middle of a fight. I owed him for all the times he promised me something and didn't come through and left me watching the door, crying on my birthday or holidays, hoping he'd walk through with a gift. On this one, particular day in October of 1999, he gave me the reason.

"STAND UP!" He said. Then as soon as I got on my feet, Dad punched me in the chest and knocked me down in my seat. "STAND UP!" He punched me again and I fell into the seat. "STAND THE F— UP!" Again, punched me in the chest and knocked me down. "YOU WANT TO HIT ME, DON'T YOU?! STAND UP! I DARE YOU!"

This time, when I stood up, my fists were balled up, tears streaming down my face, teeth gritting. I was enraged and I had made up my mind, this was it, whatever happens, happens. I looked over at my sister Sarina, standing in the doorway of the kitchen with her fists balled up, tears streaming down her face, gritting her beautiful, straight, white teeth… she was ready to go. One thing my mother taught us was to always stick together. We fight together, we love together, live together, die together, and we never let each other fight fair. Especially after getting jumped by groups of racists growing up, we had learned to destroy anything that posed a threat to a Wolfe. Ironically, my father also taught us that and his last name is Davis.

Sarina never made eye contact with me, she was staring down my father, but she saw me in her peripheral vision because when I looked at her she started to breathe more shallow and more rapidly. She was letting me know she was ready. I knew as soon as I struck, we would both attack my father and things would never be the same again. I humbled myself and sat down. Sarina's shoulders dropped and you could see her rage dissipate.

I made the right choice. I couldn't risk it. I couldn't risk Sarina getting hurt. I couldn't risk Sarina's living situation. I made up in my mind that I was leaving. We could never coincide again, my father and me. Not after this. But Sarina had a good life and stability. I already got her evicted once before, I needed to chill. After school that day, I came home and told Sarina, "I'm coming back for you, but I'm leaving. I'm running away." I didn't know where I would go but I knew if I saw my father again, we would engage in fisticuffs on sight. I packed my bag and I ran away.

Trust the Process

If my thirty-three-year-old self could have a conversation with my fifteen-year-old self, it would likely go a little something like this… Young man, you think you're bigger than the process. Once you've become bigger than the process, you stop learning. When you stop learning, you stop growing. And if you're not growing, you're dying. You think that you've outgrown your parents' tutelage. You haven't done enough or seen enough to be ready to take on the wiles of this world. You have limited life experience and you think that you're going to take that limited experience out into the real world and effectively survive?! You're not ready. You're not prepared enough to have full control over your entire life. You may make it out of the woods, but you won't come out unscathed.

There is a reason the age of eighteen has been set as the age where you are legally allowed to go out on your own and leave your parents. It is a process that you must endure. Many of us don't trust in the process. We want to skip steps. I understand, I wanted to skip steps. But when I did, it caused me major problems along the road of life. In more instances than I can count, my unconscious mind revisited something my father taught me or tried to teach me when I came across an applicable situation. I often found myself mumbling the words "Dad was right."

The process is Plant, Cultivate, Harvest. We must wait for the harvest. That's the way the process works. When an apple seed is planted, it doesn't just magically turn into an apple tree. After the seed is planted, it takes lots of cultivation and grooming of that land; some tilling must be done to ensure that apple tree grows properly. Then, even after it starts to grow, it doesn't just drop apples immediately. The tree still must continue to be watered and fed. The tree must be pruned properly until it can sustain itself and it starts to bear fruit. At that point, after the harvest, the apple tree farmer can let the tree do its own thing for a little while. But if the tree gets left alone too early and no one is properly pruning and tending to that tree, the tree will begin to die and bear rotten fruit.

Don't bear rotten fruit. Trust the process.

CHAPTER 9 - PRODIGAL SON

When I was born, my mother had given me away. AV raised me until I was a little over one year old. AV brought be back to Philadelphia to see my mother during Christmas of 1984. My mother and AV fought over me and I ended up back with my biological mother. Because of my mother and father's addiction to drugs and their absenteeism, my own family put me into the foster care system at eight years old. Six months after being in foster care, AV got me out of the system and I lived with her again. A couple of years later, when I was eleven years old, because of my refusal to follow the rules and my behavior causing problems at school and at home, AV put me back into the system. After being in a couple of foster homes and a group home, my father had gotten himself clean and got me out of the system. My father and I were like oil and water, we never got along very well; neither one of us made it easy. By the time I fifteen years old, I ran away from my father...

Knock, knock.

"Who is it?"

"It's me, AV!! It's Travis!"

And just like that, the prodigal son had returned home. AV did the absolute best that she could. She let me work; my first job was at Wendy's, the fast food restaurant. She let me play basketball for my school. She fed me, provided shelter for me and didn't ask anything of me really, except for a little bit of money to help with bills, and respect. She provided a good life for me. Regardless, if you're reading this book, by now you know me and you can likely finish the rest of this story. I was habitual rule breaker. I still didn't follow the rules. I honestly just wanted to be my own man. I felt like I was ready to be on my own and do what I wanted to do.

When I was allowed to go outside, I came home later than I was supposed to at night. I was still a problem in school behaviorally. I was fighting in and after school, talking back to the teachers and getting detention and suspensions.

Eventually, my aunt kicked me out. I was barely sixteen years old and I was homeless. My Uncle John let me live with him. Because AV took care of Uncle John after he had his strokes and entire his left side was paralyzed, it came down to either kicking me out or not having AV come over to take care of him. He chose the former. He kicked me out. This pattern of moving in with people and getting kicked out continued for the next couple of years. For the sake of brevity, I'll just put it like this, between the ages of sixteen and eighteen I was kicked out of six different homes of family members and friends. After AV kicked me out, Uncle Bruce, and Aaron's mom did. I asked, but Daryl's parents wouldn't let me live with them, they had known me all my life and they knew better. Then James' mom, Mom Bertha kicked me out. Even Lamont's parents (who were arguably the nicest people in the world) had to kick me out. EVERYONE kicked me out. In my last few weeks in Lawnside, before moving back to Philly, cousin Raff let me sleep on his floor when he could. Other nights, I'd sleep in my car.

Bertha Cobia was an angel sent from heaven to meet me in my time of desperate need and shelter me from the storm that was my life. Let me be perfectly clear: I truly mean every word of what I just said. And not in a figurative context. Mom Bertha was my angel. She only knew me as a friend of her son but she got custody of me from AV and raised me as her own son for nearly two years. I had my own room, I had a loving family environment and I could pretty much do what I wanted. I had it sweet! Mom Bertha's rules were the most lenient I had ever experienced.

For a while I appreciated her but, you know me... Slowly but surely, the deeply rooted behavioral issues sprouted up. It was only a matter of time before I was literally arguing with her, raising my voice, slamming doors and disregarding the rules. I was ungrateful and downright disrespectful sometimes. The worst thing about it, I thought I was right. Sometimes she was wrong so I figured I had the right to defend position. If she said the sky was orange, then in her house, the sky should have been orange. My responses should have been "Yes, Mom," and that should have been the end of it. But instead, I was out to prove to her that the sky was blue, the audacity! I'm embarrassed writing this. And as much as James and I love each other today, we argued like we hated each other. I honestly don't know how she did it. Dealing with the disrespect from me. Me arguing with her biological son. And just, having to go through the heartache of having to deal with my rebellion and the disrespect. When all she was trying to do is help me by making a good home and a good life for me.

I didn't understand the detriment of my actions at that time, I wish that I had. I wish that I never put her through that pain, but, I was me and it was the only way I knew to be. I honestly don't know how she dealt with it for so long. Actually, yes I do... prayer. That woman prayed and prayed. And she believed that God would bring her through. She held onto me as long as she could until my time was up, my season was over. Everything, and yes, that includes everything lasts only for a season. And once my season had come around and ended, I was gone. Mom Bertha gave me the boot.

Once I was out of Ms. Cobia's and had nowhere to go, I tried to call my father. I had hoped that the whole prodigal son bit would work in this situation. It didn't. He and Mom gave me an emphatic "NO!" Notice I had finally been able to appreciate Ms. Sharon's efforts in my life and call her "Mom." After experiencing the love of Ms. Cobia, I understood that mom was a title deserving of someone who cared for you as a mother does. Mom and Dad had decided that I could not come back. That's the price you pay when you want to be grown and on your own before your time. I had made my bed and I had to sleep in it. The problem was, I had nowhere to put it because I was homeless.

As I look back on my life and see all the opportunities that I had to do great things, to have a loving home, to save myself some of the troubles that I had to endure; I somewhat hurt for young Travis. He could have had a better life. But, at the exact same time, I am ever so grateful because had I not had those experiences, you would not be reading this book.

One day, I was watching a group of guys who I had once respected. A couple of them had gone to college on sports scholarships. One went for half a school year, and the other had gone for a year. Rumor was they failed out. Rumor was they couldn't afford it. Whatever the truth was it really didn't matter because they were both on the corner standing with guys that were selling drugs. I remember thinking to myself, I can never be them. That is such an embarrassment. There is no way in the world that I will ever leave for college and come back to stand on the corner. To me that was the ultimate failure. These guys were sports players and they had promise. They were supposed to be somebody. People looked up to them, I looked up to them and they were supposed to make our town proud. Yet, they were back on the corners with guys who sold drugs in the neighborhood.

I had gotten tired of no one wanting me. I got tired of being kicked out. I was tired of flaunting authority. I was tired of being homeless and I was tired of being poor. I was tired of being tired of things. I wanted to follow my destiny, whatever that was and I wanted to achieve my goals. I don't have some super-awesome experience or story that prompted me to have my moment of clarity. But I am grateful for that moment. For that was the moment that caused me to look at my life and realized what truly I wanted and what I didn't want.

The irony of it all was that it wasn't someone doing something great that inspired me to do great. It was actually two young men who were once doing great and fell from greatness that inspired me to do great. But I vowed I wouldn't fall. I knew that if I did not get my life together, I was going to be right back there, on that corner, just like them. Seeing these two young men, who I highly respected, who had so much promise and so much potential, fail... go from being somebody to becoming nobody in less than a year... that will never be me, I told myself. I got in my car and even though college hadn't started yet, I drove to Philly. I had to get as far away from that corner as possible.

Create Your Moment

*Some of you are waiting for your **moment** to come. Don't wait! Some of us wait and never have our moment or miss it if does just simply come. If you have that moment of clarity, recognize it as such and take the proper actions in that moment, you can position yourself on a path that propels you toward success and total life fulfillment. Conversely, if you squander it, you may end up continuing on or spiraling down that road to an unsuccessful, unhappy and unfulfilled life. But we have the power to create what we want in our lives and we have the power to attract what we desire to us. We can create our moment of clarity—that moment when you realize exactly what you want out of life and exactly what you don't want. Simply decide that you want it, and in that moment, decide that you will place yourself on your desired path.*

This is how I did it. I started by asking myself a series of deliberate choice questions, then taking some actions based on the answers. Then, I started to assess my life based on the actions I took. Then I asked myself more questions to refine my goal a bit more and depending on those answers I took more steps.

These are some of the questions I asked myself and the steps I took to get onto the path to success, happiness and total life fulfillment.

> *What do you absolutely love to do, more than anything?*
> *Does it bring you lasting fulfillment?*
> *Can you do that thing for the rest of your natural life and still be totally fulfilled?*
> *How can you leverage that thing and use it to serve others and uplift humanity?*
> *Set a goal. Define your purpose. Start BIG! So big that when people hear you talk about it, they may even look at you funny or tell you it's unattainable. Once you've set the goal, spend the rest of your natural life doing everything you can to achieve it. Once you reach it, make it more grandiose and chase that bigger, expanded goal— rinse and repeat.*
> *VERY IMPORTANT QUESTION TO ASK YOURSELF: Does your goal only benefit you? Is your goal a benefit to humanity?*
> *How bad do you want it and why? What is your WHY? What is your reason for trying to attain this goal that you have set?*
> *What will it take to achieve your goal?*
> *Are you willing to do the work necessary to achieve it?*
> *Are you willing to pay the price? You may need to make financial, social or other sacrifices in order to reach your goal.*
> *Are you willing to keep pushing on even when things appear to be not working out? If you quit, you will never know what could have been. Trust that God will help you see it through.*

"Success consists of going from failure to failure without losing enthusiasm." — Winston Churchill

Then, after these questions were asked and answered, these are the steps I took:

➤ *Ask God for what you desire. Ask intelligently: specifically, deliberately and exactly for what you want.*

➤ *Believe (have faith) that the universe will deliver to you that which you have asked and believe that you are already in possession of it.*

➤ *Start doing the work necessary to attain that goal. With everything that is within you, develop a burning desire that is so insatiable, you are laser-focused on achieving the goal and refuse to be distracted or deterred. Where your focus goes, your energy flows, and before you know it, the things you need to get you to that goal are coming your way, falling into your lap. The universe has a way of giving you what you asked for if you get on the path to get it.*

➤ *Think of your goal at the end of a long, straight path. Along this path are little crates, each containing one of the things you need to achieve your goal (plans, models, programs, mentors, business partners, investors, customers, and so forth). But, if you don't start on the path you'll never get to the crates. If you'd just start, one by one, you'll get to the crates. One by one, everything you asked for will be yours if you continuously apply the formula.*

➤ *Finally, receive what you asked for and more! Receive the blessings of the universe with gratefulness and ask God to expand upon these blessings and make it greater and more abundant.*

CHAPTER 10 - THE AMERICAN DREAM

Young, full of potential, promise and hope; I was off to college. We are all taught by either our parents or by society or both to go to school, get good grades, get a good job, right? That's the way to the "American Dream!" My American dream was a wife, two kids (a boy and a girl), a dog, a career I loved, a house with a white picket fence around it and two cars in the driveway. The American dad in my mind was a middle-class, working man, 9-to-5, sit down and have dinner, kiss the wife, kiss the kids while they're snuggled in their sheets, go to bed and do it again tomorrow kind of guy. That's what I thought I wanted and I was on my way to getting it. I was so excited. New friends, new environment and I was a computer engineering student. We were told we were the cream of the crop. When applying to universities while in high school, I figured, I love computers so why not go into computer engineering, plus that would make for a great second career choice; but, my first choice was to become a police officer.

After the first semester, I was on academic probation. I had a 1.9 grade point average and they were threatening to kick me out of school. How did I fail so miserably? I'll tell you how: lack of effort. I didn't apply myself one bit. After class I couldn't wait to get home to play "Socom II" on my PS2. I didn't study, I didn't read, I didn't do any work. I had been blessed with the opportunity of a lifetime and I was squandering it. Truthfully, my heart wasn't in it. I didn't love engineering, and it showed. I didn't perform well. Second semester, I barely got a 2.5 GPA. After that first year of failing miserably, I changed my major. A year later, same failures, I changed my major again. After another year of struggling, I changed my major one final time. This final time, I decided to stop trying to make myself more "marketable" so I could get a great job and start doing what I love.

I always knew I wanted to become a police officer, so I went into criminal justice. I began to flourish but I hadn't learned how to apply myself yet. I had lots of bad habits. I never completed a required reading as a criminal justice major. I never studied for a test. I skimmed everything I was supposed to read and yet, I still did pretty well. I loved criminal justice. It was my passion. It wasn't work to go to class anymore. It wasn't hard to do the assignments, because I loved it so much. (Disclaimer, I do not recommend this course of action when it comes to applying yourself to anything, no matter how much you love it or how easy it comes to you.) I was on a roll and I was sure to graduate now and get a police job and attain my American Dream without any hiccups. Then again, there's always Murphy's Law with that caveat we talked about earlier.

"You people and your music. License, registration and insurance card."

"What's the reason you stopped us?"

"Because your brake light is out."

"No it's not, 'You people and your music?' You stopped us because we're black."

For purposes of brevity and to accentuate the fact nothing that transpired this day is more important than my own personal accountability, I won't even tell you the rest of the story. I'll just tell you what I did.

I refused to give up my license when initially ordered to do so. I called the police officer a racist multiple times with the intent to antagonize him. I got out of the car, while he was in his, and told my friend (who was the driver) to press to brake so I could see if the brake light was *really* out. I cursed the officer and called him a racist again when I saw the light wasn't out. I refused to get back into the car when ordered. I had in my possession what appeared to be a pen but was really a Taser that I had bought from eBay for my sister.

The bottom line here is "what did I do?" Look back at every situation that you've gotten into where there was a not-so-preferable outcome for you. We are so quick to blame everyone else for the situations that occur in our lives; the teacher didn't do this, the police did that, my parents didn't do this, my boss is a... rarely do you hear someone say, "I messed up" or "I'm the problem!" In every situation, our attitude determines our outcome, either positive or negative. Will we learn from the situation? Will we lose control and take the situation to an undesirable level and get a negative reaction from the other people involved or even from ourselves? Will we learn how to deal with this situation better in the future?

In 2004, I was trying to become a police officer; instead, I ended up being arrested by one. For years, I blamed the officer and his blatantly racist comment for my actions that day. I can honestly say one thing, regardless of his feelings toward me or people of my skin complexion, had I not done the things I did, I never would have been arrested. My entire life could have been ruined in the blink of an eye because I didn't control my temper, because I didn't control my actions, because I didn't control my attitude.

If you weren't born into money you blame your parents that your life was full of struggle. You blame your circumstances and you blame your environment. But when you were in high school, what did you do? Did you apply yourself, get great grades and get a scholarship to college so you could get out of your environment? Did you learn a trade or come up with an idea for a business so you didn't have to go to college and get a 9-to-5 that entered you into the rat race? Did you work and save your money so you could invest it and let it grow and work for you after getting a financial education? Or, did you read real estate books so you could learn the real estate market and purchase/sell property so you could become the top realtor in the country? What did YOU do? You won't fix everyone else. But you can fix you. Look at you, for you are the only being that you have total control over.

Nothing I can do will change the past. The only thing I can do now is take the wisdom I've gained from those experiences and attempt to teach others how not to make those same mistakes. I can teach them how not to cause detriment to your family by making the right choices. I can teach young parents to teach their children how important it is to make good life decisions even at a very young age because the things we do, even as youth can destroy our lives or the lives of others around us whom we love. I can teach individuals not to make excuses for their actions or blame their decisions and circumstances on the actions or inactions of another.

You, and only you are solely responsible for the things that happen in your life. Your philosophy shapes your attitude, your attitude begets your actions and your actions beget the result, desired or undesired. If your attitude is one of a negative mindset you will act negatively and your results will reflect the same. If your attitude is positive, positive will be your actions and your results will be those of a positive nature.

When I became responsible for myself I began to ask myself "What did you do?" Once I started to ask myself, what I did, I stopped blaming others for all the things that were happening to me and in doing so, I learned to control my actions since I knew that I would reap the positive or the negative harvest of that which I had sown.

So, what did you do? How was your attitude? How were you thinking, positive or negative? What actions, attitudes or set of beliefs of yours caused the chain of events in your life that led you to this point? There are no accidents, there is no happenstance nor chance. Every situation in your life is the result of your thoughts, words or deeds. It's the Law of Cause and Effect. You know the old adage; you reap what you sow. Without a doubt, you have sown, so at some point, reap you will, indeed.

See it Before You See it

If you don't DREAM BIG and visualize what it is that you desire in life, which is a prerequisite for manifestation, you may never acquire it. If you never see yourself in possession of what it is you desire, before you physically possess what it is that you desire, you may never manifest what it is that you desire.

Humor me for a moment and think about Bill Gates; in all his wealth as the richest man in the world. Imagine, for a moment, what it would be like to be at that level in your life? Imagine what $1 Billion looks like in your bank account? One Billion is 1,000 millions. Now, as of February 10, 2017, Forbes listed Bill Gates' net worth at $84.8 Billion! Imagine how that would look in your bank account? See it before you see it... The difference between Bill Gates and anyone who doesn't have financial abundance is that Mr. Gates dreamed BIG, financially, but he also worked to attain the dream he dreamed, however big. Do you think he ever saw a limitation to the things he could do/have, the people he could help, the greatness he could acquire? You don't have to want what Bill Gates has, but whatever it is you want, you must dream BIG and believe you can have what you dream about. Be grateful for it now as if you already have it while also being grateful for what you have currently. Feel the feeling now that you'll feel once you're physically experiencing that financial freedom, happiness, abundance and fulfillment. You need to see it before you see it, or you may never see it.

Yes, I was told "Unfortunately we are unable to give you a conditional offer of employment at this time, but we encourage you to reapply" fourteen times. But I had already saw it. I saw myself in that police uniform helping a poverty-stricken family to stay cool in the summertime by buying them fans. I saw myself feeding a hungry little girl whose refrigerator was empty because her grandmother was too handicapped to get to the store. I saw my family being proud of me for achieving the unthinkable and becoming what I have always dreamed of becoming and I was determined to awaken one day, having what I dreamt be my reality.

Clearly Define and Expand Your Goal

All things in the universe are growing and expanding, as should your goal. Expanding your goal brings about deeper understanding. Once you expand, expand again, and then, expand again. The purpose is to make your goal as grand as you can fathom. If you can feed a nation, why would you only feed a family? If you can inspire the world, why would only inspire those close to you.

On our quest for success, knowing your ultimate goal is extremely important. Sometimes seeing our ultimate goal can be simple. We may go with our first thought or idea, instinctively. But be aware, if seeing your ultimate goal is too simple and too easy to come by, you may be thinking too small. The bigger you think, the harder you'll work and the more you'll accomplish. Not to mention, the bigger you think, as you expand upon those thoughts, your thinking gets even bigger and more grandiose—it can become cosmic, even.

Know When to Quit

Travis, you never know when to quit." I've heard that so many times in my life. Nevertheless, that statement holds true till this day. I encourage you to know when to quit on your dreams: NEVER! There are two things I can assure you of when you have that moment of doubt about your future, when things just don't seem like they're working out and that fear sets in. (1) You will experience pain and (2) that pain will not endure forever. But there is one little caveat. If you quit on your dream, your pain will endure through endless regret.

You may not become the greatest singer in the world over night. Maybe you get booed off stage once or twice because your

fear got the best of you and you held back on that high note that
you hit in the shower every time you practiced that song. But if you
keep at it, you keep practicing, you keep investing in yourself and
giving it everything you've got every waking moment of your life,
maybe you'll kill that next show—small win. Maybe you'll get a
second opportunity because you killed that show—small win.
Maybe someone records you killing the show and posts it on social
media and the world gets to see and hear you kill it—bigger win.
Maybe someone whose job it is to search for talent comes across
that video and wants to get you on TV show or a morning news
show or Ellen or Steve Harvey—even bigger win! Then maybe, just
maybe, from there, the national exposure has the A&R director
from a major record label reaching out to you—HUGE WIN! You
meet them, you kill it, you ink a deal. But if you quit when you get
booed off stage, you'll be watching other singers tell that story on
talk shows and you'll always regret you didn't keep at it.

    I played basketball in high school. I didn't work hard
enough at it, so I wasn't great. I was only 5'7" but I was the fastest
on the team. I played point guard. Although I was better than the
coach's son and his "nephew," (his son's best friend) they got
more playing time than me. I was good enough to start, but they
always started over me. I hated that. They were both slow, couldn't
play defense as well as I, didn't hustle as hard and couldn't jump. I
could dunk and I was stronger than both of them. My ball control
wasn't that good but I still felt I was good enough to be one of the
starting five.

    The one game I did start, we played Audubon Green Wave.
I will never forget it. We were in Audubon; the gym was packed.
There was some sort of tournament there. I remember walking on
the floor and all of our fans and my friends were cheering for me
when I walked on, because I never started a game before. I was so
excited to get the start and show everyone what I could do. After
the tip off, the Green Wave scored. I came down the court after the
inbound and the guy guarding me switched as another guy said, "I
got him, I got him!" as he got in his defensive position, I said to

him, "Oh you got me?!" I walked him down to about 2 feet from the 3-point line and shot a three right in his face. The crowd went crazy. "Yea Trav," "Get em Trav," "Let's go Trav," I heard from the crowd. I was absorbing it all. I had never felt this feeling before. It was like a high I had never experienced and I was addicted already.

Our next possession, they made the same switch, I shot another 3-pointer and this time I blew a kiss at the man guarding me as I shot it. I turned and walked toward the other goal before the ball even went in, I knew it was good. I was cocky and brazen. The very next possession, I passed the ball at the 3-point line, I got the ball right back and I shot it again. Another three! I was hot. Audubon called a timeout. Our coach implored me to run the play he was shouting out. Our next possession, I drove to the basket and got fouled as I made the shot. I made the following free throw and I now had 12 points. I got a steal on Audubon's next possession, and ran down the court for the layup. I scored 14 straight points. The crowd was going crazy. Audubon called a timeout. When I got to the sideline, the coach benched me. I didn't play another minute of the game!

I was furious. I was so enraged, I was blind to the fact that my actions on the court were selfish. Instead of becoming a better team player and working hard enough to get so good the coach couldn't deny me the starting position, I quit. The next year, I tried out and I was still better than the coach's son and his nephew, but I got cut. I never tried to play basketball for a team ever again.

Michael Jordan got cut from his high school team. Had he quit then, I wouldn't be mentioning his name because he wouldn't be revered as the greatest basketball player who ever lived. I'm not comparing myself to MJ, But what I am saying is, the difference between the person who quits on himself and person who doesn't, is that the person who keeps pushing and gives it everything he has every waking moment of his life, can end up becoming the greatest that ever lived. The person who quits, ends up talking about how he's not comparing himself to the greatest who ever lived.

Don't Quit!

Today, there is this epidemic where we no longer appreciate the idea of delayed gratification. We want it NOW. Instant gratification or else! As soon as we don't get what we want, we are ready to turn the world upside down and demand we get whatever it is that we wanted. We threaten, we wag our finger, we let people know they don't know who they're messing with! We tell them who our daddy is or who we know in this department and that department and we let them know we're going to have their job! All of this because we didn't get what we wanted and we'll stick with it and see it through until we get our way won't we?

Why, then, don't we do the same thing with our dreams? As soon as things don't work out the way we want them to, we quit. We've tried a thing for a few months and haven't made any money and we just give up on our dreams and aspirations, citing the fact that it didn't bring in the income we wanted. You're not going to make a million dollars overnight unless you win the lottery jackpot. You could have been right on the cusp of breaking through, meeting that 1 person, getting that 1 big break, closing that 1 deal that would have propelled you into massive success but you quit because after a year you haven't made $100,000. Stick with it, love the process, await the delayed gratification, don't quit. Your big break is coming. Stay the course and continue to grind until you get the results you want.

What If You Didn't Quit

1) Get a sheet of paper and something to write with.

2) On the top of the page write down ONE THING you absolutely loved to do. That thing that you could have done for the rest of your life and been completely fulfilled doing it but you quit at some point in your life.

3) Now, without having any limiting beliefs, write down a list or summary detailing what your life could look like if you had given absolutely everything you had to that ONE THING you loved to do and never gave up. Describe in detail the things you'd have, the places, you'd see, the money you'd earn, the people you'd help, the lives you'd save, the changes and innovations you'd bring to humanity etc. Imagine for a moment that you worked on this ONE THING like Michael Jordan worked on basketball, like Johann Sebastian Bach worked on compositions, like Bill Gates worked on Microsoft or Picasso on painting, like the greatest in your field works on his/her craft.

For another thirty seconds, continue, to envision how great your life could've been right now had you not quit.

Now, maybe you haven't experienced these things (just yet) in your life, but the good thing is, you can absolutely have everything on that page! If you're breathing, you're still alive, so you can still do it. However many years ago you quit doing that ONE THING, those same amount of years are going to pass again. When they do, you'll either be in the same place you are today, or, conversely, the things you're reading on that list you just made, you can make them your goals. You can decide to finally do that ONE THING you absolutely love to do, work at it with an insatiable desire to achieve it, and NEVER QUIT. One, three, five or ten years from now, you'll be closer to having everything you want on that list. But I can assure you this, if you don't do that ONE THING, you'll be plagued with endless regret, forever wondering what could have been if you just did it.

Do that ONE THING, experience your American Dream and finally have the life you've always wanted.

CHAPTER 11 – NO MEANS YES

We have been taught all our lives that "No means no!" Luckily for me, all the way through my teenage years, I was a habitual rule breaker. To me, no means yes! Every time a police department told me they weren't going to hire me, I kept pressing on, kept trying, kept applying. Every "no" got me closer to a yes. Every "no" encouraged me to push forward. And one day, my tenacity and my determination to achieve my goal finally paid off. On February 9, 2007, I got my big break. It was Friday afternoon, around 1pm. I was at work, in between classes, when my cell phone rang. Someone from the Philadelphia Police Department was on the line. They told me to report to the academy on Monday morning, February 12, 2007 at 8am. "So wait, I'm hired?!" I asked with a surprised tone, yet trying to be cool like I expected it. "Yes. Monday at 8," she said with a stern voice, "and you should arrive early."

I could not hide my emotion. I was happier than I had ever been in my entire life. I had finally landed the dream job that I always wanted. Officer Wolfe! Officer Wolfe!!! I was in my last semester in college and I had just four classes left. The semester would be over in a few months. While logging in on the computer to drop all my classes, I called my family up to ask them what they thought I should do. Everyone, except one person, said that I should finish school. "You can always get a job but this school thing is a once in a lifetime opportunity." "Only four classes left, you can take the job next year." "If you leave school, you'll never go back and finish."

Two things were obvious: (1) These people had absolutely no idea what I had gone through all these years when it came to getting a police job. (2) They didn't know it, but they just gave me the fuel that I needed to drop out of school, complete the police academy and go back and finish school. I dropped those classes, gave my current boss a handshake and thanked him for everything.

He let me leave a half hour early that day and didn't dock my time. I was out, but in seven months, I'd be back!

In September of 2007, right after I finished the police academy, I enrolled back into college at Temple University and took two classes a semester. I graduated within a year. I wouldn't be denied. I had become determined not to lose, no matter what! I was the father of two, Diana and I had been engaged and we were having some relationship struggles because I wasn't devoting enough time to her and my family. I was determined to keep my family together. I was trying to be a good husband while I chased my ambition of becoming a police officer while also trying to finish college. Balance was difficult, absolutely, but it was made possible by my willingness to want to have balance and succeed.

The academy was a breeze. I paid attention in class and soaked up information like a sponge. I barely had to study. I loved learning law. I graduated amongst the top in my platoon in grade point average. My platoon sergeant was new at the academy. It was his first platoon and he was very proud of it. He was fond of me and told me that I would make a great cop but "You know what?" he said, "You'd make a better sergeant."

He once told our platoon that I would be his first ever recruit to make the rank of sergeant. I believed that I would be. And because of the power of personal belief, the same department that denied me employment in 2005, hired me in 2007 and then promoted me to sergeant in 2013. I am my academy platoon sergeant's first recruit to make the rank of sergeant.

At twenty-nine years old, I decided that I wasn't fulfilled in my career as a police officer and I wanted to serve on more of a grand scale. I decided to pursue my dream of joining the US military. My old police partner, Sean helped me train before I went to the Army's Basic Combat Training because he said I wouldn't be able to keep up with the eighteen-year-old kids. That was all the motivation I needed. He knew I could outdo them but he also knew how to tap into my competitive spirit. I was already in decent shape, I just needed refinement. When I first got to basic combat training, I heard a bunch of people talking about how they were going to be the platoon leader and how they're going to get a perfect score on the PT test and this and that. I was quietly motivated to shine in every area.

At first, I couldn't attain the coveted perfect 300 score on the Army Physical Fitness Test. I didn't get the max score in the two-mile run and I was missing the sit ups max score by about fifteen sit ups, but I was determined. Every night after "lights out" I would roll out of bed and do sit-ups until I couldn't sit-up anymore. Then, I'd do more sit-ups.

Eventually, I became the first pick for platoon leader also known as platoon guide (PG) in my platoon. One particular drill sergeant, from a different platoon, appeared to hate me. She seemed determined to get me fired as PG. She told me almost daily that she was going to have me fired. She intentionally did things to try to screw me up and to make me look incompetent. Every other platoon had hired and fired multiple PG's. It's what they do. The intent is to break you down and build you back up the Army way; build great Army leaders. But I would not be phased or deterred. I was a great leader. By the end of basic training, I was the oldest PG, the only one that didn't get fired and replaced. I crushed the sit-ups that plagued me early on and when the two-mile run got difficult for me in the last two laps, I thought about my why—my family. I wanted to make them proud. I couldn't let my son down. I wouldn't be able to look Travis, Jr. in the face and have him see me as a failure, knowing that I quit on myself in that run. I had to dig deep! Leaders lead from the front! I achieved a 300 score on the Army Physical Fitness Test and I graduated with honors. I garnered the respect of my peers and the drill sergeants, alike all throughout basic training. I solidified the idea in my mind that I could accomplish anything I wanted to in my world.

Every time I was told "no," or I am not expected to be able to do something, it's fuel for the fire that is my burning desire to succeed. People's disbelief in me is a greater motivator than people's belief in me. Knowing the odds are against me is invigorating. I've had the odds stacked against me my entire life. This is my arena. I'm the champ in that game. I thrive in it.

I have always taken pride in the fact that I was a leader. I was a leader in school. I was a leader of my family, in college, and amongst my peers as a police officer. Then, I had proven my leadership capabilities on the highest level—in the greatest army in the world. In the Army's officer candidate school (OCS), I proved it again. My leadership in the police department still resounds throughout the department today. Growing up, I wanted this job more than anything and I was so proud to represent my family and my department in my work. I always wanted to be a leader in the department. To be a thing, you must become that thing. Dress like it, talk like it, act and do like it. The first thing people say when you ask them about Travis Wolfe (if they don't say he's the consummate professional and leader) is that he was always the best dressed and most professional looking and acting in the district, maybe even in the department. Maybe I'm embellishing a bit. Nah. Whenever there was a detail where the department needed a poster boy, a staunch representative of the level of professionalism that the department embodies, I would get calls from the offices of the bosses asking me to take the detail. Especially if there was a photo-op.

My chief inspector's office contacted me when they needed a sergeant to represent the department as the Special Olympics flame of hope came through Philadelphia on a UPS airplane. I got presented with awesome opportunities to meet and take pictures with some of the world's greatest athletes because I look, think, work and act in a professional manner always. I even got a chance to volunteer with the US Special Olympics afterward because of the connections I made during this opportunity.

If you happen to be in North Philadelphia, west of 10th Street, and you happen to find the most squared away police officer in the 22nd police district, I likely look a little better in uniform than him/her. Whenever the local news got a 1-5 second clip of me on a crime scene, I would get flooded with phone calls and text messages from people in the department telling me how "sharp" or "squared away" I looked. People would often ask me if I was in the military (before I was even in the army) just because of how I carried myself and wore the uniform. In 2008, when I came to the 22nd district; which I will assert manufactures and grooms the best officers in the entire department, the appearance of most the officers left much to be desired. Not many had much pride in their appearance—not often wearing the 22nd district collar pins, not having clean uniforms, shined boots, not being clean shaven every tour, etc.

The bosses (the top brass in the department) always wore collar pins, they had their boots shined, they had clean shirts all the time and theirs were white! Their shirts were pressed and their trousers were neat and clean, not baggy, tattered or dirty. I always admired the current commissioner of the Philadelphia Police Department, Richard Ross, Jr. The consummate professional. Always looking like he just stepped out of a police department magazine or a photo shoot. He was as sharp as a tack in his appearance and wit. He was always one of the most respected members in the department, even before he was commissioner. He is a great example of how officers should maintain their appearance and a model for a stellar police career. Like I said, if you want to be a thing, you must become that thing. If you want to be a leader you must become a leader in your talk, thoughts, actions and appearance.

I always had my shirts tailored and military creased. I shined my boots before, during and after the shift if I got dirt on them. My duty rig was shined and could be used as a mirror if you needed to comb your hair or check to see if you had something in your teeth. I wore every pin allowable by policy. Griff, one of the cops I used to work with, would compare me to Brian from the movie "*Office Space*." Griff would say, "Wolfe, you've got all thirty-seven pieces of 'flare' on today, I see." People would say I look slike a police recruitment poster. I was constantly complimented on my appearance by my peers, my supervisors, bosses in the department and the public. I became the professional I wanted to be.

I acted like I was supervisor before I was one, I learned what supervisors had to learn to get promoted, I read and studied my departmental policies daily, I looked at calls that I handled from the perspective of a supervisor instead of just an officer. Because of it, when situations would get difficult, oftentimes my peers would call me for answers, especially when it had to do with policies. They would ask for my advice on situations before they'd call a supervisor even if it was policy to call a supervisor. They jokingly called me sarge, lieutenant and sometimes captain and would say to me "Don't forget about me when you become commissioner, you'll need a driver!" I was still only an officer at that time.

Once, an irate woman who was refusing to listen to any of the officers on a particular scene asked for a supervisor. The officers called me over to handle it. I was just an officer but I looked the part and knew the part of a supervisor well. By the time it was all over, I had handled all the woman's concerns professionally and quelled her frustrations. She was satisfied and didn't require any further service.

Today, not only in the 22nd district, but throughout the department, I see individuals dressed how I dress. Tailored shirt, pins on the collar, shined boots and rigs, tailored pants, etc. Eight years ago, this type of appearance was not as prominent as it today. By being the best possible example, impressing my peers and supervisors with my appearance, by 2011, I had changed the culture and brought pride back to how we wear our uniforms. Now more and more officers wear their uniform as I do. Although my claim could be debatable, if you ask an officer who was in the 22nd district from 2008-2013 "who was the best dressed officer, they'll mention my name. And if you ask them did anyone dress the way I did, before I came, they'll be hard pressed to think of anyone.

Remember I said you must become that which you want to be? By 2013, that belief and attitude had proven true as I was soon to be promoted to sergeant! When I asked the commissioner (then deputy commissioner) for some advice for a young soon-to-be sergeant, among the things he told me, he said to continue to stay sharp in my appearance. He added, "leaders lead by example; because your appearance is always professional, you're a good example to follow. Treat your officers with respect and never tell them to do something that you wouldn't do yourself."

The horn tooting wasn't meant to point out the fact that I am a well-put-together individual. Although admittedly, it feels a little like humble bragging telling the story. Nevertheless, the purpose of that story was so that you could understand that when you become in your mind what you desire to be in the world, you become in the world what you see in your mind. I became a sergeant in my mind before I experienced it in the natural world, and eventually I became in the world what I saw in my mind. By becoming what I wanted to be—dressing, talking, acting and doing like the sergeant I wanted to become—I am now a sergeant.

He Who Thinks He Can
and He Who Thinks He Can't are Both Right

Confucius said, "The man who thinks he can and the man who thinks he can't, are both right." Think you can, and you will. If you or someone else says you can't and you believe it, then you won't. Because someone said you can't, that's exactly why you must. You know what you can't do? You can't afford to let yourself down again. You can't afford to have your children unable to focus on their education because other kids are making fun of them for wearing the same clothes they grew out of the year before last. You can't afford to have your children wondering why their life isn't as good as others. You can't afford to have your children growing up thinking that being poor is just the way life is supposed to be. You don't have to be poor. You don't have to be considered underprivileged. You can't afford to keep feeding your children and yourself unhealthy fast food because you believe that's all you can afford. You can't afford to have the people you love watching you die on a hospital bed because your heart couldn't handle the aftermath of twenty years of abusing the dollar menu. You can't afford to keep day-dreaming at work, wondering "What if." What if I had, what if I could... what if you just believed that you could and went all in instead of just wondering "What if?" The person living her dreams and achieving her goals is not special. She is not lucky. She just believes she can, and so she does. And so can you.

I once decided I would achieve this "American Dream" that I had deigned in my mind, which consisted of a house, two cars, a wife, two kids, a dog and a white picket fence. I believed I could achieve it and I took whatever actions and did whatever work was necessary to get it. Seven years later, I bought my first home. I had my house, my wife, two kids, two cars, and I bought a dog. Then, to complete what, at that time, was my idea of the American Dream, I bought my white picket fence. I had the career I wanted and everything else I imagined and believed I'd one day have. I was the American dad.

"When you become in your mind what you desire to be in this world, you will become in this world what you see in your mind."
— Travis T. Wolfe

Have a Personal Development Regiment

Your personal development is absolutely critical to your success. Sometimes as humans we appear to get worn down, tired, sometimes we get distracted and sometimes we need encouragement. Sometimes, we get frustrated when the path gets difficult, we get tired of fighting for what we want and when we hear no, it means no—and that's a no-no! Personal development keeps us on the right track and helps us bring ourselves back when we've gone down that dark road of negative thinking. Through personal development, you will find the tools that you need to stay a self-motivated self-starter. A personal development regiment consists of listening to, watching or reading inspirational, motivational and empowerment audio, books or videos. You should also consider reading at least 10 pages of a good book every day. One that is going to motivate or empower you or give you knowledge that you can immediately apply that will help you get to that place in your life that you desire to be. Go to seminars and workshops that will help you stay motivated and inspired. Don't be afraid to invest in your personal development.

I have 19 Apple products in my home, two PlayStation 4's, multiple large televisions. I've spent tens of thousands of dollars on "stuff" and I'm totally embarrassed by it and disgusted with myself. I used to be proud of it, like I had accomplished something by buying "things," none of which added any value to me as an individual. I would quickly buy the latest iPhone or latest "Call of Duty" for PS4 but I wouldn't spend a dime on a seminar about real estate or the stock market or empowerment or anything else. The moment I realized how detrimental this behavior was to my pocket and my growth, I started to invest in myself as opposed to investing in things that had no ROI (return on investment). A personal development regiment will give you infinite return on your investment and will help to take you to the next level in your life, something "things" just cannot do.

That same personal development that I invested in helped me to believe that I could start my own company, gave me the knowledge on how to do so and helped me build a network that supported me on my journey. Something "things" and "stuff" just cannot do.

Once I decided to start my own company, and become a professional speaker, every day I worked on myself. I worked on personal development and self-education. Jim Rohn, one of the greatest motivational speakers/trainers of all time said "Formal education will make you a living. Self-education will make you a fortune." Oh, and was he right! I had my formal education, and I had my living. I couldn't apply my college degree to make me any more money than I was already making. My overall professional growth had pretty much maxed out unless I passed a series of tests and got a promotion. Those opportunities were scarce. With Jim Rohn's quote in mind, I studied for hours upon hours, learning about the speaking industry. I searched for gaps that I could fill with my unique perspective and style of speaking.

I woke up early, between 3 and 4 am every day and immediately went to work using my personal development tools. I read at least ten pages of a good book that was going to edify me. I listened to great speakers like Dr. Eric Thomas, Tony Robbins, Les Brown, Grant Cardone, Zig Ziglar, Bob Proctor, Jim Rohn and many, many others on YouTube and podcasts. I would listen to e-books in the car instead of music or talk radio stations. In the world of personal development, we call that "Drive Time University."

Investing in yourself is another major key to your success. It is part of your personal development journey and you must not skimp on it. Spending money to go to seminars or trainings and getting coaching is necessary if you really want to take your life to that "next level." Stop buying "things" making someone else's dream come true by helping to make them rich and wealthy, and instead, invest in yourself and your dreams and make **you** rich and wealthy.

I implore you to read *"The Slight Edge: Turning Simple Disciplines into Massive Success & Happiness"* by Jeff Olsen. This is the book that helped me to get onto the path to success. It has helped millions to get on and stay on the path to success by teaching you the importance of applying simple disciplines to decision making and time management. I also implore you to read *Think and Grow Rich by Napoleon Hill.* Everyone who is anyone who is successful, especially financially successful has read that book or at least applied its principles. *Think and Grow Rich* has changed my life and the lives of millions of other people and I am certain it will change yours.

CHAPTER 12 - KNOW WHO YOU ARE

I used to simply be the son of two drug-addicted parents. Once a product of an impoverished environment and the foster care system. I was abused, molested and raped by the time I was eleven years old. I was once a habitual rule breaker, and because of it, I was kicked out of multiple homes. I used to think I was a failure. But the truth is, none of that defines me. In spite of all my perceived detriment, challenges and hardship, I AM a child of God. I am a survivor. I am a success, I am a dreamer, I am an overcomer and I AM GREAT!

The good thing about knowing who you are is that if you don't like who you perceive yourself as, you can become the person you wish to become. We all have the ability to define ourselves and redefine ourselves. If you're lazy and would rather sleep in, rather than grind and hustle and develop your skills and abilities as an individual, and you want to change that, you can. You can replace any quality you perceive as undesirable with one that you prefer. That's the beauty of it. Even if you, admittedly, haven't been the greatest person you could have been up to this point, you don't have to settle for mediocre. Replace those negative qualities with great ones. Start with your mindset. If you don't have a positive mental attitude, you'll allow negative influences to plague your mind—developing a negative mental attitude and essentially stunting your overall growth.

I often found myself involved with the law. My Nana planted the seed and I watered it. I gave power to her words by choosing to allow what she said about me become truth in my life. I chose to give it that meaning. If you adopt someone's belief about you, if you give attention and energy to what people say about you, you will become exactly what and who they said you are. We become that which we believe we will become and what our focus is upon.

As a youth, we believe almost anything our family tells us and I believed my Nana. My behavior reflected my belief. I became someone who did the things that would land an individual either dead or in jail. I was seven years old when I first got arrested. Police involvement in my life was normal. When my dad assaulted my mother, the police were there. When my mother would steal from stores and get caught, the police were there (they'd usually let her go because she would have four kids with her.) When I set a fire to the leaves in someone's backyard, the police were there. When I broke a window with a rock, yep, police. When I stole from the Heritage's on Broad Street, in Woodbury, police. And when I stole the water guns from Kmart...you guessed it, police. When my aunt stabbed my other aunt, more police.

All this police involvement and I was barely eight years old. I look at my son and I find it hard to believe that what I'm saying about my police involvement could be true. I had to verify it with my mother, father and Tiona. My son has never had a personal negative experience with police. By his age, I had about 25 police interactions. There is no way that I could even imagine my son leaving the house alone to go to the corner store and he's ten years old, right now. I was stealing from the corner stores, walking almost a mile to school, stealing bikes or scooters when I didn't feel like walking and breaking into people's sheds and getting arrested by the age of seven! It's amazing what exposure can do to the mind of a child.

I often wondered why individuals who come from affluent neighborhoods, financially successful families and upper class tend to do well in life and why individuals from more impoverished neighborhoods with less financial means, and lower class, poor families don't normally do as well. Granted, there are socioeconomic challenges, racism (institutionalized and other) and other systemic injustices that play a role in the success/failure rates of individuals. But I have found that individuals predisposed to success have an easier path to success and ones who are predisposed to poverty, tend to adopt the idea that poverty is just a way of life and they learn to accept it. Without desiring more out of life, they can easily accept the status quo. When you have, or create opportunities to experience or just to see more, it can be easier to dream for more or desire more. Although I grew up at the lower end of the class spectrum, and I was so poor I didn't even realize it was poor, I just accepted life for what it was… terrible… I eventually found that I wanted more out of life and I went after what I wanted. Poverty isn't permanent, unless we've developed a poverty mindset and have chosen not to change our mindset. If we desire more, we can be more, we can have more and most importantly, we can give more.

I recall a line from the book *Success Through a Positive Mental Attitude* by Napoleon Hill and W. Clement Stone, and it reads: "We shouldn't be poor and don't ever let me hear you say that it is God's will that we are poor. We are poor not because of God. We are poor because father has never developed a desire to become rich. No one in our family has ever developed a desire to be anything else."

The same works with everything else in your life. If you adopt someone's beliefs, you will adopt their reality. If you adopt the beliefs of the poor man, you will be poor. Conversely, if you adopt the beliefs and behaviors of the wealthy, that you will become. If you think about poverty, and how it's affecting you, you will be poor. If you think about abundance, success, fulfillment and how these can change your life, you will have abundance. Earl Nightingale, one of the fathers of the philosophy of success and one of the world's greatest thought leaders made famous, the saying, "We become what we think about." The truth is, you can find this principle in the bible and other religious texts and you'd be hard pressed to find a truer statement.

"You're a failure!"
"You're a loser!"
"You're stupid!"
"You're just like your mother."

"You'll never amount to anything."

Either you've heard these things from other people in your life or you've said them to yourself. And guess what?! They're all true! That is, once you believe and accept them as your reality. The amazing thing about the unconscious mind is that it doesn't know the difference between what is real and what is imaginary. It does not discern fact from fiction. It believes exactly what you tell it and then a compilation of all that it believes is what forms your philosophy.

Your philosophy begets your actions and your actions beget your result, positive or negative, desired or undesired. If you continue to tell your unconscious mind that you are poor, by believing it you are indeed speaking it into existence in your life and the universe must manifest what you think and speak in your personal life. Therefore, yes, you are and you will be "poor." As Sigmund Freud theorized, your unconscious mind is the primary source of human behavior. Therefore, believing you're poor will cause you to unconsciously act as if you are poor. You will live like you are poor. You will spend, eat, talk, think and do as you are poor.

Fortunately for us, the unconscious mind operates the same way when you tell it you're a success, you're a winner, you're smart, you're going to amount to great things. Keep telling your unconscious mind that you are going to be a millionaire ten years from now and you'll be one. But wait, don't go running around shouting from the top of the highest mountain thinking great success will come to you just yet. There is one small caveat, well two, actually. When you say it, you must believe it **and** you must be willing to do the work necessary to become one. You didn't think it was that easy, did you?

Before I understood any of the above, I had a poverty mindset and I hadn't yet been exposed to anything that would allow for me to want or desire more. Then, along came Mr. Arthur. Mr.

Arthur told me I was better than that. He told me I was better than I or anyone else believed I was. There was something about this man that made him trustworthy and believable. I believed him, and for the first time in my life, I became better.

Pastor Jeff Arthur was a devout man of God. He assumed many roles at my high school, Haddon Heights, in Haddon Heights, NJ. He was a hall monitor, security guard, substitute teacher, a great mentor to many and likely one of the most liked and favored people at Haddon Heights High School. He had a way of making you believe that you could be better than you were. He would encourage me, knowing I was going through tough times. He knew I had promise and he always told me that I did. He would give me money for lunch a couple times a week, at least, to make sure I could focus on my school work and not my stomach being empty. After meeting him, my junior and senior years were my best years in school ever, behavior-wise.

Mr. Arthur continued to impress upon me the importance of education and made sure I met the application deadlines for colleges. He also made sure I maintained my grades and kept out of trouble. He would come and sit in my classes just to make sure I was behaving. Pastor Jeff was like a father to me. He was inspirational, he was motivational, he was Godly and he loved me as a person regardless of my perceived faults.

Mr. Arthur had me over his home and let me see what a family was supposed to look like. He showed me a different environment, one that I could dream of one day creating for myself. He taught me to believe that I was worth something. Worth being loved, worth someone's time and worth taking a chance on. I had to make him proud. I got myself laser-focused and graduated with a high GPA and got accepted into multiple universities. I did that for me because I wanted better for me, of course, but part of me did it for him, to make him proud, to show him he didn't waste his time on me. Had it not been for him, I may not have dreamed of better for myself and pursued anything better than what I already had. I finally knew who I was.

Environment is Everything

As I mentioned before, it's amazing what exposure can do to the mind of a child. I expose my children to arts, I expose my children to high ideals and success. I let my children know they are a child of God and through him they can do all things. I expose my children to goal setting and goal achieving. I expose them to honor and integrity and love and compassion for all people. My fifteen-year-old daughter is a philanthropist, owner of a production company a film director and filmmaker. She's already made two short films and is set to release her first feature length film this year, 2017. She was fourteen when she filmed it. As far as our research has shown us, once complete, she would be the first fourteen year old in America to ever write, direct, film and edit a full-length feature film.

My son is a ten-year-old philanthropist, dancer and actor. He's won 5 high point gold medals at the United States Tournament of Dance, one of those high point gold medals was for a solo. By that point, he had only been dancing for two years. He's been in many commercials, movies and television shows.

By my tenth birthday, I had more police encounters than the combined numerical total of both of their ages put together. My environment and exposure was different. I would never expose my children to the things I was forced to be exposed to. Not surprisingly, neither of them have ever had any negative police interactions. It's amazing what exposure can do to the mind of a child. It's obviously no secret that I am happy for the accomplishments of my children. It's also no secret that one of the secrets to success is placing yourself in an environment conducive to achieving and succeeding. If you live in a poverty-stricken environment and you don't make the decision to change your environment, you can fall victim to the beliefs, opinions and ideals of those in that environment. And because of the limitations believed to exist in such an environment, you'll begin to subscribe to the perceived lack of opportunities in the world. Nevertheless, if you change your poverty mindset to a "success is the only option" mindset also known as a success consciousness, you'll see opportunity and possibility in everything. You'll also expose yourself to desirable environments that afford your mind the chance to imagine, envision and to dream of success, achievement and fulfillment.

Whether, like my family did, you live in a roach infested, low-income housing complex or you live in suburbia, once you're exposed to an environment that lets you dream, you can dream BIG! No longer do we need to see joining a gang or selling poison to the community as our only options. No longer do we have to get a gun and "hold down our block." Once we've been exposed, we can dream and if we can dream it, and believe it, we can become it.

"What the mind can conceive and believe, the mind can achieve."
— Napoleon Hill, Think and Grow Rich

O.S.A. - Objective Self-Assessment

So, you want to know who you are?! Great, you've taken the first step to becoming successful. Before you can go any further, you need to perform an Objective Self-Assessment—O.S.A. Conduct a truly impartial, honest and unbiased self-assessment so you know exactly who you are.

Entrepreneurship is popular today, it appears, especially with millennials. It seems now, everyone is an entrepreneur, or trying to be one. Being responsible, I feel I must address this. If you're an entrepreneur, you're not a 9-to-5 kind of person. But, if you love 9-to-5 work hours, entrepreneurship may not be for you. Lots of us don't fare so well in the entrepreneur world and don't understand why. If you don't like to get up early in the morning and work, if you love sleep more than you want to be successful, the entreprenuer life may not be for you. If you love hanging out in bars more than you love hanging in your office, building your brand and your company's income, the entrepreneur life may not be for you. You must be ready and willing to break off relationships with people who can be poisonous to your success mindset. You must be ready to miss some family events. You must be willing to invest in self-education and personal development. If you're not willing to do these things, then become willing to or try a different path, other than that of an entrepreneur.

If you find that you're a 9-to-5 kind of person, be the best 9-to-5er there is so you can get to the top of your company. Be the best at whatever it is you do so you can get to the next level in that arena. Don't stay stagnant. Don't lie to yourself and convince yourself you're completely happy and fulfilled where you are. If you're not taking on more responsibility, you're not growing and if you're not growing, you're dying. What people fight the hardest for in this life is to stay alive. We do whatever we have to do to ensure we live and don't die, it's instinctive. So, instinctively, you want better, you want more, you want to grow! If you've convinced yourself you don't, you're lying to yourself. You're likely scared. Fearful of progress and what it will look like for you. Fearful of hard work or more skills that you'll need to attain which will call for more studying or more hours at work. Whatever the case, you want more even if you have convinced yourself that you don't because we must grow, or we die. Be honest with yourself in your O.S.A. Know Who You Are!

When you conduct your O.S.A., if you do not like what you've discovered, understand that you can change. You don't have to be what you've found yourself to be. When conducting this Objective Self-Assessment, the purpose is not to find yourself, but rather to DEFINE YOURSELF. Become whatever it is that you wish to become.

Your Objective Self-Assessment

On a separate sheet of paper, complete an Objective Self-Assessment. Ask yourself and answer these questions honestly.

- ➤ What type of person am I? (List as many self-descriptive attributes you can think of.)
- ➤ Am I currently happy with my life?
- ➤ Am I "successful" by my own definition. Remember, although success is subjective, success in any particular area of your life does not constitute overall success.
- ➤ Am I a 9-5 type of person or an entrepreneur?
- ➤ Do I want to climb the corporate ladder or am I comfortable in a mid or entry level position?
- ➤ Am I a go-getter or a wait-for-it-to-come-to-me type of individual?
- ➤ Does it fulfill me more to give of myself, time, finances, physical labor, gifts, help, etc.,) or to receive something from someone?
- ➤ Employer or employee? AND does my work ethic match?
- ➤ Do it myself or pay someone to do it for me?
- ➤ Am I an artist, into visual, performing, culinary arts, etc.?
- ➤ Do I love formal, institutional education or do I prefer self-education?
- ➤ Do I love to teach or prefer to be taught?
- ➤ Am I a positive individual or do I carry negativity with me?
- ➤ Do I love to serve? Do I love to give?

These are the types of questions that are important to ask ourselves. One of the most important things we can do is to find out who we are. Without first knowing who you are, you cannot properly plot out the right course and decide the action steps you need to take to get you closer to your life's goal. The good thing about knowing who you are is that you're also able to define who *you are not and you can immediately decide to become that which you wish to be.*

Together, "I AM" are the two most powerful words in the English language. When said, whatever follows is a proclamation and accepted by your unconscious mind as truth and fact. In an article titled "The Power of I AM," written by Dr. Wayne Dyer, he explains, "The words I AM, which you consistently use to define who you are and what you are capable of, are holy expressions for the name of God—the highest aspect of yourself."

I implore you to be prudent when you use the name of God and associate it with something that God is not. When you constantly tell yourself, "I am unhappy," you're right, in one sense. You told yourself you are not happy and so, you won't be unless you change the language you use when talking to yourself. Instead, try stating "I AM happy." When you consistently imprint on your unconscious mind the idea "I'm experiencing happiness" you will experience happiness. Conversely, if you imprint on your unconscious mind negative or any other limiting statements or beliefs, such will be true, just the same. If you want to affirm a thing, and manifest it in your life, let it be positivity, happiness, success and fulfillment, not the adverse.

If you don't know who you are, anyone can tell you who you are and it'll be who they believe you to be. If your self-esteem and self-belief is weakly rooted and your opinion of yourself is too malleable, anyone with limiting beliefs and a lesser opinion of themselves or you can possibly project their fears and beliefs on you. If you're not careful, you can adopt another's beliefs and opinions about you and that will become your reality. The better you know yourself, the more impenetrable you become.

WHO ARE YOU?

*Below, or on a separate sheet of paper, write down everything you are and desire to be. (example: loving, punctual, happy, smart, a great singer, a great author, etc.) NOTE: If using a separate sheet of paper, at the top, in **BOLD** and CAPITAL letters, write the words "I AM"*

I AM

CHAPTER 13 - KNOW WHAT YOU WANT

After running away from my father and being kicked out of six different homes of family and friends from the time I was fifteen to eighteen, I had to take an honest look at my life. I was free falling without a parachute and I could see the rocks below. I pulled the string, but, nothing happened. I pulled the reserve, but to no avail. I hadn't yet hit rock bottom but I could see it, and it was quickly approaching. I looked in the proverbial mirror and that's when I finally saw myself. I was a stud! After I got past how much the women would swoon over this devilishly handsome 18-year-old face of mine, I saw my demise. I saw myself hit those rocks if I continued down that path.

I didn't want to end up going splat. I wasn't going to end up a failure like so many either told me or expected of me. I wanted to chase my dream of serving in the military and becoming a police officer and living out my American dream. In that moment, I asked God what I had to do to get the things that I wanted. And for the first time in my life...I saw vision. I saw promise. I saw my future. I finally knew what I wanted.

I didn't want to be the guy who dropped out of high school and sold drugs on the corner. I wasn't a loser, *I WANTED TO WIN.* I didn't want to work at Wendy's and McDonald's all my life. My manager fired me from Pathmark because I gave a poor woman and her kids a cooked chicken without ringing it up. I didn't want to be poor and need a free chicken. My Nana often told me that I would end up dead or in jail just like my father. I didn't want to be my father. No one wanted me. Everyone I've ever had in my life had abandoned me and I alienated myself by refusing to follow the rules. Well, I didn't want to break the rules anymore. I had become determined not to lose no matter what and in turn I had learned HOW TO WIN!

What Do You Want?

Before you can have what you want in life, first thing's first...
KNOW WHAT YOU WANT. On the next page, or on a separate
sheet of paper, write down everything you desire to have in your
life. (Example: happy family, financial freedom, happy marriage,
promotion at work, to start your own company, etc.) After you've
written down what you want, revisit your "I AM" list. You should
find that your list of what you want reflects who you are. If what
you want is inconsistent with who you are, you may want to rework
*the lists to find harmony. Remember, **you don't get out of this life***
***what you want, you get out of this life what you ARE**. Become*
what you want, and you'll have what you desire.

Read instructions on previous page before making your list.

I WANT

Become it!

"A tree doesn't get the fruit it wants; a tree gets the fruit it bears."
— Les Brown, World Renowned Speaker and Author

An apple tree will always bear apples. No matter how bad it wants to bear oranges, it can only bear apples. You're an apple tree (a lazy employee), but you want to bear oranges (make CEO money). Well, you're going to have to plant a different seed, my friend. You're going to have to become that CEO you wish to be. You must walk like a CEO walks, talk like a CEO talks, do what a CEO does and wear what he/she wears. You must think like he/she thinks, believe like they believe, grow like they grow and then, you'll become a CEO. It won't happen overnight, for sure, but after you plant and cultivate those seeds, one day you'll wake up and there'll be oranges at your feet and you'll look at yourself and you'll see that orange tree and you'll say to yourself... "I have arrived." You'll drink your cup of fresh squeezed orange juice and you'll go on your way, off to work, to the top floor at your company, the CEO suite.

You don't get out of life what you want, you get out of this life what you are. Become what you want to be. If you want to be a survivor, become a survivor. If you want to be a winner, become a winner. If you want to be the person who makes $200,000 a year, become the person who makes $200,000 dollars a year. Do, act, think, grow, learn and believe as the survivor and the winner and you can become a survivor and a winner. Now, I'm not saying there is some cookie cutter way of overcoming your victimization or addiction or trauma. And of course, the road is easier for some than others. But if you are willing to work at it, and if you are determined to become that thing you want to become, (an overcomer, a survivor, a success, etc.) regardless of the amount of work it may take, regardless of how hard you may perceive it to be, *regardless of any obstacle; if you decide to be resilient, disciplined and determined, I profess to you, nothing is unattainable.*

If you want to be a successful owner of a company, become that person, NOW! Emulate what that person would do on a day to day basis, surround yourself with successful business owners that can teach you and show you what they do to be successful so that you can emulate them. You have to be that person mentally, see yourself as that person, before you will ever become that person on the physical level.

If you want to be the greatest player that ever played basketball, you have to become the greatest player that ever played basketball. Find out what the greats have done to become great. Do that. Maybe even do more! Your desire should consume you to the point of obsession. You should want it with such a burning desire that you can taste it. You have to want it so bad, that it's almost all you do. If you couple your insatiable desire to become great, with a positive mental attitude and apply the necessary effort; that greatness will be yours.

CHAPTER 14 - KNOW HOW TO WIN!

Winning is not simply something you do. Winning is a mindset. Winning is a quality, a character trait that you embody. A winner is not someone who has won something. A winner is someone who develops within themselves an attitude and a culture of achievement and success through a positive mental attitude. Winners can lose and turn that loss into a win regardless of what the record books say. Winners can find the win in all situations. Winners do not know failure by the average man's definition. To a winner, "a failure" is not capitalizing on an opportunity to learn from a situation, win, lose or draw. To win, you must become determined not to lose. In doing such, you force yourself to learn and gain experience from every situation, which is, in itself, a win and a success.

$$(a + b)(x) = success$$

You cannot just simply imprint success on your unconscious mind and lay on the couch waiting for it to come to you. As soon as you imprint success on your unconscious mind, it begins to go to work on how it can get it for you; but you'll still need to do the action(s) that will manifest the desired results. Imprinting success on your unconscious mind means you've told yourself over and over that you're going to be successful (whatever that looks like to you.) Your unconscious mind believes it and accepts it as fact. You truly see it in your mind's eye and you believe it and act as if you already have it. However, your unconscious mind doesn't have the power to manifest the things you want in life. **It is your actions that are responsible for manifesting the things you desire.**

Your unconscious mind shapes your paradigm. As Steven Covey explains, in his book *"The 7 Habits of Highly Effective People"*—your *paradigm* is how you see, perceive and understand the world. Your unconscious mind also shapes and develops your philosophy and is therefore directly responsible for the thoughts that cause your actions. Action *must* be taken in order for anything to be manifested. Action moves the once stored energy, that energy builds momentum and momentum pushes you closer to your goal. Be deliberate and specific and ensure that your actions are congruent with your thoughts, emotions, dreams and words. Then, as Ralph Waldo Emerson says, "do the thing and have the power."

Your compensation and your reward will be of equal measure as your contribution. The measure at which you perform a service, help someone, love someone, give to someone, etc., by that same measure will you be compensated. More popularly, this is known as and relatable to the adage "You reap what you sow." It is the Law of Compensation and the Law of Cause and Effect.

It would be irresponsible of me if I did not add this caveat. Yes, as explained, for your actions based in love and positivity, you will be compensated, for certain. Equally, for your actions based in anger, doubt and fear, you will be compensated. Your reward, positive or negative, will be in exact proportion as your contribution.

As you read this chapter, open your mind, like never before. Open your mind to the possibility that maybe, just maybe something here may be exactly what you needed to help you get started, or help you get over the hump. I didn't always believe the things I believe now. I didn't always understand things the way I do today. I didn't always know what I know now, but I wish I had. If only I had an open mind all those years I deliberately denied myself the opportunity to learn something that could help me get to a better place in my life. I wish I didn't dismiss everything educational as "mumbo-jumbo." I wish my poverty mindset didn't lull me into thinking I was doing fine just as I was and I didn't need any new knowledge. I wish I didn't assume being successful was so "hard" and called for so much "work" that I refused to take a chance on myself.

Today, I am thirty-three years old. I didn't go all in or give 100% to ME until I was thirty-two. I wasted 1/3 of my life. When was the last time you went ALL IN for YOU?! If you know you've never even given yourself a full 100%, Take a chance on YOU! Don't watch others who have achieved their dreams, wishing you had their life. Those people, whose lives you admire, they came from where you are right now in your life. They just took a chance on themselves. They went all in on them! They kept their mind open, absorbed knowledge and applied it. You can do the same. Go get that life you dream about! Have the life you've always desired! You deserve it!

If you apply the following formula and principles to your life, I am certain that you'll begin to see positive change. You'll begin to see things differently and things in your life will get better for you. But you must make the decision that you will have a better life. Decide to finally give 100% to YOU. That's not a lot to ask of yourself. Stop quitting at 70 or 80%, claiming you gave it your all. You owe yourself more. A.L. Williams wrote a book entitled *ALL YOU CAN DO is ALL YOU CAN DO but all you can do is enough.* If we aren't where we desire to be in life, then we haven't done enough. Don't do 95%, do enough. If you don't have what you want, you haven't done enough to get it. Do enough.

a — Ask

"Ask, and it will be given to you; seek, and you will find; knock, and it will be opened to you." —Matthew 7:7 (ESV)

You've heard it a thousand times throughout your life, not even realizing that it's actually part of the blueprint to your desired success, achievement and fulfillment. Ask, intelligently, deliberately, specifically and exactly for what you want. The universe must give you what you ask for. There is great power in getting in tune with the universe, a higher power. Some call it "Source," some call it "God," some don't call it anything. And I'm not judging or challenging your beliefs, so whatever you call, or don't call it—just ask for what you want. I implore you to take this

116

step as it is truly the first step in attaining any lasting success in your life.

b — Believe

"Now faith is the substance of things hoped for, the evidence of things not seen." —Hebrews 11:1 (KJV)

Be•lief — noun.
trust, faith, or confidence in someone or something.

Belief (faith) is powerful. Think about this. Think about where you are in your life right now. This very moment. How many times, since you were a child, have you been told that **this** is where you'd be? Your parents may have told you that you would go to school get good grades, go to college, get a good job, find a mate, get married, get a home, have children, etc., etc. Wherever you are in your life, the idea was once presented to you, either by you or someone else. You believed in your own mind that it would be your reality and then you created the circumstances to get you here. I was always told I would end up dead or in jail. I ended up almost dead and I had many run-ins with the law. At 18 years old, I changed my beliefs about my life and where I'd end up and I began to pursue the new life I pictured for myself. Just two years ago, at thirty-one years old, when I looked at my life, I realized that I had amounted to what I believed I could. But now, I truly wanted more. So again, I had to change my belief of what my life could be.
To change the reality of your life, you must change your belief. I know you've heard it before throughout the book. My editor said it's repetitive—but repetition is the mother of all learning and such a statement warrants repetition. I cannot impress it upon you enough. I've lived it and I've seen it work. I went from being poor and riding in the back of police cars to bringing in over six figures annually and my main source of income currently comes from riding in the front of police cars. I once hated my life, my

relationship was on the rocks, I wasn't happy and I played video games for 15 hours a day as I wallowed in my own self-pity. Eventually, I followed this formula of $(a+b)(x) = success$, and well… you're reading my book.

Without challenging your existential beliefs, observe the simple process of belief and the power therein based solely on the power and ability of your unconscious mind. The unconscious mind controls your actions and infallibly it ensures what you say and what you do are consistent with what you have trained/programed your mind to believe. Your unconscious mind knows only what you tell it.

One of my best friends of 24 years, Daryl had been diagnosed with plantar fasciitis, which is a disorder that causes pain in the foot that usually is at its worse with the first steps of the day. Daryl ran track in high school and he was awesome at it. But after years of running track and playing sports, he started having foot issues. Every morning when he would get out of bed, he would plant his foot down and experience excruciating pain as soon as his foot touched the floor. One day, his wife suggested he pray and try asking for what he desired, which was for the pain to subside. Daryl never went to church. He wasn't even sure if he knew how to pray or where to start. But he did it. He asked for the pain to go away in his foot. He believed that it would work. The next morning, Daryl woke up as usual. But, it wasn't until he had gotten into the bathroom that he realized that he was in the bathroom, and that he walked there and hadn't experienced any pain in his foot. The pain he expected to feel every day when he got out of bed was gone.

When I was in college, I made only $12,000 a year. I met my wife, we had children and I had to support my family. Indeed, this was a challenge on only $12,000 a year (before taxes). I asked the universe to allow me to be a great provider for my family, I told myself I was a great provider for my family and I believed I would experience being a great provider. I was willing to do what it took to become that great provider. The next year, I earned more than 4x that amount. Today, I am very comfortable with my ability to provide for my family.

Believe that what you ask for will be given to you. Then, *act* as if you already have it. For example, if you desire to be a wealthy realtor and you ask the universe for such favor to attain that goal, you *must* believe that it will come to you. Otherwise in your mind you do not believe that the creator can bestow such blessings upon you and your unconscious mind knows this. Therefore, your actions will be those of one who does not believe he can be a wealthy realtor.

My little brother, AJ once told me that he wanted to be a real estate investor. He had no real savings and zero knowledge or experience in real estate. I taught him this same formula, he applied it, and within 5-6 months he had already placed bids on multiple properties he wanted to invest in. Because he followed this formula and imprinted on his unconscious mind that he was a great real estate investor, he began to act and do as a real estate investor does. His unconscious mind began to go to work to make him a great real estate investor and consciously, he began building a new wardrobe with professional attire, so he could look like a real estate investor. He started reading books about how to buy and sell property, the stock market and he learned how to leverage all the knowledge he gained. By applying that knowledge, it became power. He used that power to build momentum and that momentum propelled him to success. He consciously began to place himself in the presence of other realtors and investors and like a sponge he absorbed their knowledge and practically applied it. Before he knew it, he'd placed a bid in on his first property. In March of 2017, he made settlement on his first home. A homeowner, at 20 years old! No inheritance, nothing left behind for him from dead grandparents, just pure belief and a willingness to do the work after he asked for what he wanted. By April 2017, less than a month later, he had multiple contracts out on different homes, wheeling and dealing in the real estate game.

"The universe supports the reality of your beliefs absolutely.
When you believe you must struggle for abundance,
then it will bring about situations that are conducive to struggle;
when you believe you cannot experience love without pain,
the universe will give you exactly that - love with pain;
when you believe it takes time for an illness to heal - then so it will.
There is not a single force opposing you, there is only ONE force
supporting you absolutely.
It is called LOVE, the force that birthed you, that created you in its
own image.
This love is so magnanimous it will give you exactly and absolutely
whatever it is that your reality entails.
Change your beliefs and you change your reality."
- Author Unknown -

(x) — Action

Maybe you've heard about the Universal Law of Attraction, visualization and manifestation, and even the importance of positive thinking. Having such knowledge is great! But, factually— you can be the most positive person, try to visualize, attract and manifest until you're blue in the face—without implementing the Universal Law of Action, you'll just be blue.

One of the most major keys to success is action. Your knowledge, ideas, hopes and dreams are likened to potential energy—they have the potential to do great things but they do nothing until they are acted upon. *Action* is necessary to release that potential energy, essentially unleashing your thoughts, ideas, hopes and dreams with great force and momentum allowing them to manifest. The type of action you take and the faster you take it, the more momentum you build, and the faster and easier your goals come to fruition.

Begin moving in the direction of your desires by taking the necessary actions to get what you desire and you'll see, things will just begin to happen for you. Doors that you never thought were there will open for you. People to help you, money you need, ideas you never knew you had—they will all begin to come to you as you continue taking action. You may not know every action to take right now, but once you begin taking action, you'll discover the next step and the next and before you know it, you're experiencing the success you've always wanted.

To Recap:

Ask—Ask intelligently... specifically, deliberately and exactly for what you want. Properly putting our desires into the universe is necessary so that they will manifest.

Believe—What you've asked for, believe and accept that it is already yours, and see yourself already in possession of that thing. The universe will give you what you asked for when you have faith that it will. Be grateful as if you have already received what you've asked for. You must create in you the feeling of gratitude for that which you believe is yours although you have yet to physically experience it. This shows true faith, which is needed to manifest what you desire. As we know Hebrews 11:1 (KJV) tells us that *faith is the substance of things hoped for, the evidence of things not seen.*

Action/Work—This is the "x factor" when it comes to success. You must be willing to act and to do whatever is necessary to achieve your goals. That (x) represents *everything else* you need to do other than ask and believe. You will know what those things are as soon as you begin to do the work. They will come to you. All the imprinting in the world will not supersede the Law of Action. The Law of Action must be enacted in order for us to manifest the things that we want in our lives. For our desires to be met, we must take necessary action that supports our ideals, thoughts and goals.

(Ask + Believe) (Action) = Success.

I'd be doing you a disservice if I didn't explain that it's not as easy as simply applying the formula. Understanding and applying the formula is critical, but there are many other major keys to "success." And I assure you, if you apply the formula *and* apply the following principles, you will immediately begin to see positive change in your life and you'll quickly be on that path to success, happiness and total life fulfillment. If you choose not to apply these principles, or the formula, you may find that to your detriment, you will be essentially taking the long road or the scenic route to success. You will eventually learn that you must apply it all. You can learn now, or like me, you can learn later. It's up to you how soon you begin to achieve your success. Let's start now!

I.I.A. - Immediate Imperfect Action

You've heard it before, "knowledge is power." Such a statement alone, is completely false. The entire statement is actually, "The application of knowledge is power," or "Applied Knowledge is Power." It is not good enough to simply read and acquire knowledge. You must apply it, act upon it for it to become power and useful to you.

As the saying goes, "Imperfect action is always better than perfect inaction." We all love to show how much we know. We love to read ten books just to say we read them. I know you've heard this one before, "I've read the bible cover to cover!" Well, congratulations, sinner! No matter how much you read, if you don't immediately apply the knowledge you've gained, you are just as well off ignorant.

Once you have attained knowledge from any place, i.e. books, people, etc., remember the principle of I.I.A. Take Immediate, Imperfect Action. Don't wait! Immediate imperfect application of any knowledge acquired is 10x better than reading 10 books cover to cover and implementing nothing you've learned.

I used to love to have conversations with people and find that we had similar knowledge, either from a book we both read or

122

something we both heard someone say. But as I got wiser, the more I spoke on the things I *knew*, the more I realized I wasn't applying the knowledge that I professed to have. I began to question how it was that I read about and had the knowledge on how to become successful, yet I wasn't successful by my own definition.

Some of us are going to seminars and Super Saturdays all the time, coming out pumped up and excited, ready to take on the world. But, by next week, once the adrenaline stops pumping and the excitement wears off, we find we are sick with a case of the Mondays, and it's Thursday. Our business or our life is just as bad off or worse than it was before. Or what's worse, we start applying some of the knowledge and then we get discouraged by the work we realize we must put in. Or we have an experience that causes a setback (which we deem a failure) and we psych ourselves out telling ourselves it's too much or too hard, defeating ourselves and quitting before we begin to build up the momentum needed to get us that unstoppable downhill roll.

Continue on! Don't quit on that thing you know deep down in your heart you love to do. Gain knowledge in that area, then immediately apply that knowledge *consistently.* Don't wait to have perfect understanding of the "who, why, when, where, and how", as perfect understanding only comes with continued and consistent application. Consistently continue to apply that knowledge and continue taking Immediate Imperfect Action until that imperfect action become perfect action, and that perfect action translates into success.

Give

Everyone has his #1 key or secret to success. My #1 not-so-secret "secret to success" is giving, because without giving not only will your success not be fulfilling, it will not be sustainable in the long term. Furthermore, the measure at which you give, is the measure which it will be given to you.

"Give, and it will be given to you. A good measure, pressed down, shaken together and running over, will be poured into your lap. For with the measure you use, it will be measured to you."
— Luke 6:38 (NIV)

I'm not just talking about surface giving and giving of things, but, rather, giving of yourself in every aspect. Your time, help, finances, energy, efforts, labor, ideas, etc., are all different ways in which you can give of yourself. Helping others get what they want in life is a guaranteed way to get what you want out of life. Zig Ziglar, once, one of the greatest salesmen, speakers and authors often said, "You can have anything you want in this life if you help enough people get what they want. If you're not getting enough, you're not giving enough."

Anthony Robbins, currently one of the best speakers/trainers in the industry of speaking/training, often says, "the secret to living is giving." Personally, I have found that giving has been one of the top reasons that I never truly want for anything. God seems to always bless me with everything I need and everything I ask for. When I was a student at Temple University, I said earlier, I used to make only $12,000 a year. I was working 39 hours a week while a full-time student and I had to take care of Diana, Aniya and Travis, Jr. We had two cars, a house that I rented for $750 a month and of course normal living expenses, cell phone, cable, etc. The rent alone was $9,000 a year. Math was never really my strong suit but the math just doesn't seem to add up. I couldn't afford to live on that income, but somehow, I never was kicked out for non-payment of rent and we never truly had trouble making ends meet. Was money tight? Certainly, but we never went hungry. We may have eaten Oodles of Noodles for dinner some nights, but our bills were paid and we always had our needs and even our wants met.

I believe we were always given what we needed and wanted because we have always been givers. I have always given of my time, my attention, my finances, etc. I have always given of my total self to others, especially when they were in need. You've heard the saying, "you reap what you sow," another Universal Law. The universe must give back to you that which you put out. When you do a thing, that action is energy and that energy that is sent out must come back to you.

Some time ago, my checking account was negative, my savings was at zero, and all my credit cards were almost maxed out. I came across a woman in need of some financial support. I wanted to give her something to help her out a little. I searched my wallet, and had no money. I went into my secret "stash" for emergencies in my car and found five $1 bills. I gave what I had left to the woman. I believed that God would provide for me and my family what I needed to make it through at least until I got paid again the following week. When I got home, an hour later, I checked the mail as I always do when I come into the house after noon (which is around the time our mail gets delivered). In the mail was a check that I had expected to come more than forty-five days prior. Being dead broke at that time, the amount of the check was a relatively large sum for me. It was in the five-figure range. Now, I am not telling you that if you give your last $5 you'll receive a big check. What I am saying is that, if you give of yourself the universe must give back to you according to the measure at which you give. It may not always happen right away, but if you give, God will give unto you, for it is the law of the universe.

Change Your Attitude

Your circumstances and your environment are reflective of your attitude. Your situations, your income, the friends you have, the clothes you wear, the job you go to, the car you drive; all of it is an exact representation of your attitude and essentially shapes who you are as an individual. Change your attitude, change your life. A negative mental attitude attracts negative circumstances, and when those negative circumstances come about in our lives, what do we do? Do we complain, cry, make excuses, tell ourselves "nothing ever goes right for me?" That essentially brings on even more negativity. If we have a positive mental attitude in every situation, we will attract positivity to ourselves. We will see the positive and extract the positive in all situations. Our attitude determines the outcome of every situation.

> *Always turn a negative situation into a positive situation.*
> — *Michael Jordan*

How many times have you heard someone say "I had to hit rock bottom for me to see my problem, fix it, and turn my life around..." If you had the power and ability to pick yourself up at rock bottom, you could have picked yourself up before rock bottom. Why wait to hit bottom before you changed your life?!

You could have turned your life around before you lost your children, before you lost your home, career, wife/husband, etc. Why did you wait?! Attitude. **Attitude is everything**. If you have a "woe is me" attitude, yes, absolutely, woe is you and woe will continue to be you until you change your attitude. And, for some of us, change doesn't come until we hit rock bottom and associate so much pain with our life's circumstances that we are forced to choose to change our attitude.

Attitude determines the value of the experience. If we have a negative attitude when we try to start a company and things don't work out, we'll likely accept that experience as a failure. We may wish to consider accepting it simply as an experience that will help propel us past a similar situation that will come our way in the future. That experience helps us learn how to overcome. And now we know exactly what not to do next time when we try our hand at business again. Equally, we'll be able to take away the positive things that worked for us so that we can duplicate those things next time and expand upon them. With the right attitude and mindset, we can understand and interpret failure for what it truly is. I always say *"What is perceived as a failure should be perceived as simply an experience that ultimately contributes to your success."*

Know you will "fail." Accept it and embrace it. The phrase "Failure is not an option!" sounds amazing. It can fire your team up and push them to play harder than they ever have, but what do you tell them when they lose—after you just told them that failure is not an option?

Failure absolutely is an option, but it's what you do with that failure that can turn it into a success and an invaluable experience. You fail your way to success. Winston Churchill reminds us that *"Success consists of going from failure to failure without losing enthusiasm."* If you accept your failure as a "failure" then, you will likely become demotivated and there may be no enthusiasm to continue to push forward.

Naturally, if you're one that accepts failure after you fail at something you'll quit. But if you quit, you lose and you will never know what could have been. That is why we must have a different attitude toward "failure" and our definition of failure must change. To me, failure is simply an invaluable experience and an invaluable lesson learned. My belief is, either you win or you learn and you succeed or you learn. I welcome "failure," because every "failure" (invaluable learning experience) gets me closer to my success, closer to my win!

I did not fail. I successfully discovered 1,000 ways not to make a lightbulb. — Thomas Edison

Redefine what "failure" is to you. Attempt to turn the negative associations with failure into something positive so that when things don't necessarily go as planned, you may still find value in the situation and learn something from it that you can benefit from in the future.

FAILURE IS:

CHAPTER 15 — GO BE GREAT!

As the man with the gun moved his finger onto the trigger and slammed the barrel of the handgun against my teeth, he ordered me to take him and his partner in crime upstairs to my apartment. For the final time, with my arms extended out to my side, touching the wall on either side of the stairwell, keeping them from getting upstairs, I told him "No."

My sisters were up there; and these men would have to kill me before I let them upstairs and hurt my sisters. The second man, his partner, urged him "c'mon, man, let's go," but he refused. Instead, he glared directly into my eyes with a look that pierced my soul as he said to me, "I should blow your f— head off!" At that moment, I knew I was about to die. I found myself praying to God for mercy, hoping I'd be delivered.

Throughout my life, I had been told NO more than I was told anything else. I was told NO, don't do that; NO, you can't be; NO, you can't have. Being told "NO" motivated me to get what I wanted even more. I had always believed that I was supposed to be "dead or in jail, just like my father" but I decided to stop giving any power to such a belief. I believed that my life wasn't supposed end with me lying dead on the stairwell in my apartment building. I believed that my destiny was greater and that I could control it, shape it, design it—by deciding to. All my life, I had defied authority. I defied my parents and I defied my foster parents. I defied my aunt, my teachers and my friend's parents. But, now, I wanted to defy the odds.

There are no accidents in life and nothing occurs by happenstance. The drug-addicted parents, my drunken father abusing my mother, the foster homes, the abuse, the molestation, the rape, the group home, the church, running away from my father, getting kicked out of homes, the homelessness, sleeping in my car, sleeping in the woods, facing death multiple times in my life… When you realize that things in this life happen *for* you and not *to* you, you look at your situations differently. You'll be grateful and appreciative of your situations knowing that they are making you stronger so that you can become the person that you're supposed to become.

Every situation you endure is happening for you—so you can gain the experience needed to get you to that next level in your life. It happens to make you stronger; to build up your confidence to show you that you have what it takes to move forward in every endeavor. Situations in your life are happening for you, preparing you for what is to come.

Until I learned how to overcome a negative experience with a positive mental attitude and learn from it, turning it into a positive experience, I continued to have negative experiences. Everything has purpose, you included. You're supposed to go through these tests, they build character. The trauma, the loss, the experiences you wish you never had, they've built resolve, strength and character. You're supposed to use your life's experiences to help others get through theirs and help them build character.

Yes, I had some troubling and traumatizing experiences, but don't pity me. Had I not had the circumstances I had in my life, I wouldn't be able to help others who have had the same or similar circumstances. I wouldn't be a published author. You wouldn't be reading this book. I wouldn't own WolfeMpowerment Group. I wouldn't be speaking to groups of people empowering them to walk in their purpose, overcome all obstacles and win in every facet of their lives.

My father once said to me "Son, your pride will be the death of you. And if it's not your pride that kills you, your mouth will be the death of you." Proverbs 18:21 says *"Death and life are in the power of the tongue."* Had I continued to believe what my father told me, he would have been right. But I was going to defy the odds. I stopped believing that my tongue would be the death of me and I tamed my tongue. Now, ironically enough, not only do I speak life into my personal situations and my own life, but I speak life into the situations, circumstances, and lives of others.

Thanks to the character building circumstances that God has allowed me to overcome, people know that my character is battle-tested, tried and true. They know that my character is one of integrity, honor, trust, empathy, honesty, positivity and high moral standards. You know where I come from. You know the type of life that I've lived. If I can come from where I came from, do the things that I'm doing, and accomplish what I've accomplished, you can do, have and be whatever it is that you so desire in your life.

"If you become in your mind what you desire to be in this world, you'll become in this world what you see in your mind."
— Travis T. Wolfe

You are supposed to be here. You are supposed to be successful and fulfilled. You are supposed to WIN! With all that you've been through in your life, you must know and believe that for you, there is a greater purpose. You must see it before you see it. You must act as if you already have it. You must be grateful for it and ask God to expand upon it! You already have greatness within you. You don't have to find yourself, you were never lost; define yourself! Know who you are and know what you want. When you become determined not to lose, that's when you'll WIN! Success and greatness are in abundance and are yours for the taking. Go get some—and Go Be Great!

WHAT PEOLE ARE SAYING ABOUT TRAVIS

Travis Wolfe has always been someone that I look to for real world advice. One of his greatest attributes is that Travis is never judgmental. He uses his experience and mistakes that he has made to share advice that comes from the heart. Travis has shared life lessons with me that I hold on to until this day. He has a passion for helping people and that passion makes him a great role model.

— *D. Hall, Long Island, NY*

Mr. Wolfe's speech was incredible. It was inspiring, touching, and revealed much about the determination of this man. To come from the literal ashes and become the person he is today shows just how much willpower he has. He has always been a measuring line of what I wanted to be. This speech has made me admire him more so.

— *T. Miller, Philadelphia, PA*

Travis did an excellent job when I heard him speak. His message was so powerful it had the whole room teary eyed. You can feel his words as he tells his story. It motivated me to be appreciative with what I have. Also, it showed me that if he could make it under those circumstances then nobody else should have excuses. All in all, it was a phenomenal speech. It truly was an honor hearing him speak.

— *A. Perez, Darby, PA*

When I heard Mr. Wolfe speak about his past, as he compared and contrasted the 'youthful' Travis Wolfe to the amazing gentleman I know today, I was truly touched and inspired. Mr. Wolfe reminded me, through his speech, that "your past does not define you, but rather it reminds you of where you've been. Therefore, you will always be going places, as long as you Keep Going!! Your ability to create new life experiences will increase each time you aspire to Greatness."

I am a Mental Health Professional, and I understand that each new endeavor begins with a good philosophy and a proper mindset; however, it is easy to become complacent when you focus on helping others to the detriment of yourself. Mr. Wolfe's message, and the intense delivery of it, touched my heart immensely, and motivated me to keep my dreams in the forefront of my mind as I continue to use my gifts to inspire the people I work with. I transfer skills to clients on a daily basis, and since I've heard Mr. Wolfe speak of his own achievements, despite trials and tribulations, I will intentionally transfer those same skills to myself in order to achieve new levels of success.

The delivery of the speech kept the crowd engaged and excited, and it also helped convey the power of his story. Travis Wolfe is a promising orator, and I was blessed to be in the presence of Greatness!

— *R. Williams, Woodbury, NJ*

Never did I expect to receive the level of support and professionalism that Travis Wolfe provided. We spoke just about every day leading up to our event. Travis wanted every detail to be perfect! I can tell you that it was well worth it. Travis and his team provided our children with one of the most memorable presentations I have seen in my 12 years at the camp. I know

Travis and his team had a positive impact on the children. Their message is one that the kids will not soon forget.

I would absolutely recommend WolfeMpowerment Group for any motivational speaking engagement!

— A. Dorosz, Oxford, PA

Brother, you inspire me in so many ways. When you graduated college, you inspired me. I was good seeing you accomplish your goal. That one time when we were in Philly and we saw those kids smoking weed on their steps and you went to talk to them about it; I was just thinking that I wish more people were like you and took the time out to educate the youth instead of bashing them. And of course, you're motivational speaking inspires me all the time. I'm so blessed that God placed you in my life brother! I love you, bro! Just writing this about you has inspired me to go do something. Let me take these pajamas off and get dressed.

L. Roman, Portsmouth, VA

I TRULY THANK YOU FOR READING.

IT IS MY PRAYER THAT YOU TAKE
SOMETHING AWAY FROM THIS BOOK
THAT WILL EMPOWER OR INSPIRE YOU TO
GO BE GREAT!

Notes

Notes

Special Thanks:

Carleton Crispin –Technical Director, WolfeMpowerment

Carleton, I am truly grateful to have you as a friend and thankful for all you do. I appreciate your tireless hours of dealing with my insane meticulousness with great patience, while consistently producing quality work. I thank you for your dedication and I appreciate you and your family's trust and belief in me. Your character, attitude and work ethic are amazing. You're a great man, C! I AM grateful to have you on the team. I love you, brother.

WolfeMpowerment
GROUP

· Inspiration

· Motivation

· Empowerment

·Transformational Leadership

Go Be Great!
Overcome and WIN!

Travis T. Wolfe

www.wolfempowerment.com | info@wolfempowerment.com

267.816.8244

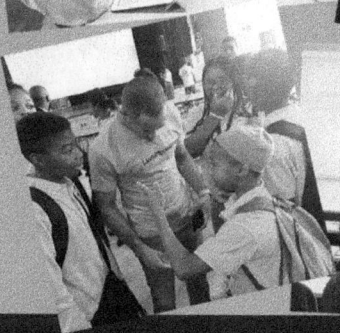

141

TRAVIS T. WOLFE

**Uplifting Humanity by Empowering
and Inspiring All to Go Be Great!**

Speaking
Coaching
Consulting
Mentoring

*"When You Become In Your Mind
What You Desire To Be In The
World—You'll Become In The
World What You See In Your Mind"*

www.wolfempowerment.com | info@wolfempowerment.com

267.816.8244

142

What Does Success Look Like to You?

www.ingramcontent.com/pod-product-compliance
Lightning Source LLC
Chambersburg PA
CBHW070447090426
42735CB00012B/2484